Morning Glory's
FARM FOOD

Stories from the Fields, Recipes from the Kitchen

TEXT BY GABRIELLE REDNER | PHOTOGRAPHY BY ALISON SHAW

A Martha's Vineyard Cookbook

VINEYARD STORIES
Edgartown, Massachusetts

Published by Vineyard Stories
52 Bold Meadow Road
Edgartown, Massachusetts 02539
508-221-2338
www.vineyardstories.com

Library of Congress Number: 2014940648
ISBN: 978-0-9915028-3-7

Book Design: Jill Dible, Atlanta, Georgia

Printed in Canada

FOOD, GLORIOUS FOOD

By Prudence Athearn Levy, Founder, Vineyard Nutrition

I love vegetables and fruits. And this is probably not an ordinary love or one primarily fueled by their nutritional virtues, however vast. I simply love them.

Growing up on Morning Glory Farm, I'd get just as excited about a ripe strawberry as a friend might get excited about an ice cream cone. Pulling carrots out of the earth, feeling the snap of an English pea, and listening to the sound it made as it plunked into my wooden basket, these are the things that shaped me, built my childhood, and forged my relationship with food. When I look into the center of a bright green broccoli plant, shrouded with robust leaves, I think perfection. Nature's perfection and farming perfection, all wrapped into a gift of versatility, sustenance, and nutrition.

Farming with my family is really the reason I became a nutritionist and registered dietitian. From a young age, I've wanted to share this beauty, this offering, with others. When I decided to turn my passion into profession, vegetables and fruits had enriched my life where I knew I had to share this knowledge with others.

Today, we're seeing a surge of public interest in supporting local farms, eating more fruits and vegetables, and home gardening. But we don't need a trend or current research to tell us what our taste buds already knew: freshly picked, locally grown produce tastes better.

And fruits and vegetables are certainly beginning to take the limelight. Kale is featured on the menus of the best restaurants from New York to California. Daikon radishes, purple carrots, purple potatoes, kohlrabi, Long Island cheese squash, and heirloom tomatoes are all taking turns on the expanding stage where previously only broccoli, peas, and carrots stood. Chefs love them, and consumers are happy.

We are now seeing vegetables in their glory, not just as a side dish covered with butter, but a celebrated, delicious, integral part of the meal.

We are now seeing vegetables as food.

There is no doubt local foods taste better, and are better for the planet, and most likely are better for us. Our typical supermarket fare includes foods that may have traveled over an average of 1,500 miles. Fewer miles from farm to plate means farmers can harvest at peak ripeness. For the consumer, this enhances cell structure and vitality of the plant, translating into crispness, succulence, and flavor. Smaller farms that grow for quality, not simply production, can choose heirloom varieties, experiment with new crops, use people instead of machines for harvesting, rotate crops for soil nutrition, and practice sustainable, if not entirely organic, farming. On the protein side, grass-fed beef, free-range chicken, and locally raised pork all outshine their mass-produced counterparts in nutrition quality, safety, and composition.

Morning Glory's Farm Food takes you behind the scenes, giving an insider's glimpse into how farm fresh food is raised and who is raising it—including other farmers on the Vineyard. This book highlights crops from inception to harvest, offering recipes chock full of delicious, fresh ingredients for you to cook with a new appreciation for the complexity and the quality of the food you are using.

NEW FIELDS FOR AN ISLAND FARMER

Jim Athearn, Farmer

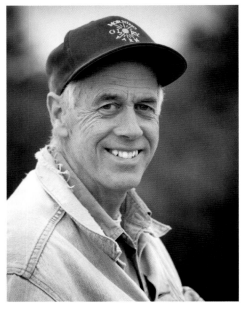

Since I returned home to become a farmer in 1973, I have enjoyed walking in the footsteps of my Island ancestors, as well as countless generations of other farmers, who have turned the soil with a plow, dried hay in the June sun, admired green rows of healthy crops, led cattle to green pastures, and sat gratefully at a family table laden with foods drawn from our own lands and waters. I have felt a common bond with the men and women from all centuries who have worked hard and experienced suffering and joy from living with the forces of nature.

After forty years of thinking I was living in the past by my stubborn insistence on agriculture as my living and lifestyle, I am now finding I am not alone. All around me are people defining the future through small farms, living locally, and appreciating the simple goodness of fresh, pure food. I see this in the way my two sons and daughter are raising and feeding their own children, in the scores of enthusiastic applicants asking for work on our farm, in the vibrant West Tisbury Farmers' Market, and in the new small farms popping up on Martha's Vineyard. Eating local food has generated a new word, locavore, while across the nation food buyers are asking where and how their food was grown.

To be honest, we have always had people wanting local foods since we first set up our planks and sawhorses by the side of the road to sell vegetables. Through the years I frequently heard stories from our customers about how they visited their grandparent's farms and enjoyed the lifestyle and food. However, these were also the first generations to reject farming for a living. They had come to believe there was no money in farming, and that the only food possible was from mass production on large farms. They got used to the supermarket quality of tomatoes and corn. They forgot what a good, fresh vegetable tastes like. Our customers, who have for almost forty years gone out of their way to buy fresh vegetables, were the exception, not the rule.

Many years ago, I ate in one of our local restaurants where the carrots—not my carrots but cheap ones from off-Island—were served as an afterthought to the entree and were tasteless mush. I thought, "These cooks do not respect the vegetables." More recently, my daughter, Prudence, then a vegetarian and now a nutritionist, expressed great delight in the taste of some simple vegetable. I marveled that she could get so excited about a mere vegetable and realized that I, too, did not respect my vegetables, not the way she did.

I began to really taste each vegetable, unadorned with butter or salt, and now I know they are indeed equal partners to the meat on the plate. I could make a meal of sautéed shallots and bok choy now, if there wasn't so much other good food to enjoy. I also began to appreciate their nutritional value.

I've realized: You can live on this stuff!

Like a converted agnostic, I want to preach to the world, "Respect your vegetables!" I want more of our customers to enjoy beets, Napa cabbage, and, of course, bok choy. This is one of the themes of this book and through these pages we are hoping to bring people a little closer to full appreciation and respect for our great home-grown foods—and the work and love that goes into them.

It was a great surprise and joy for me when our sons Simon and Dan wanted to join us on the farm. They've added new thoughts, energy, and excitement. Yet since the beginning we have been blessed with talented, dedicated employees who have contributed to our farm culture. Many have continued to work in agriculture after they have left us.

The Athearn family of Morning Glory Farm, 2014

And many of the employees today reflect a growing interest in farming. They are serious about learning the technical skills of farming—about soil structure and chemistry, bio-controls, and cover cropping. On Chappaquiddick, four bright, educated men and women, led by Lily Walter, created a new farm from scratch on rolling land and unimproved soil. All veterans of our own farm, they have the experience and energy to make it work. Other young people, either new to the Vineyard or raised here, are launching serious ventures in food production.

Some of them may have picked up some lessons from Morning Glory Farm, but they have also created a new community of forward thinking farmers. They may be motivated by media buzz about the local-food movement and a recognition that people who work the land are to be respected. But this newly vitalized acceptance of farming as a way of life is reflecting what I believe is a universal desire to work with the land to feed ourselves. Chefs and food writers have it right: they want to use what's grown close, and they know it tastes better. Local farms are the focus of it all.

I feel stirrings of excitement as I discover new fields of learning and improvement opening up for farmers today. In particular, I am excited about discussions of soil health and how new methods of tillage and cover cropping, combined with better soil tests and more precise balancing of crop nutrients, can lead to healthier, more productive crops with less fertilizer. This year we have started growing some of our corn and pumpkins using no-till methods. Daniel is experimenting with ways to grow strawberries that don't get swamped with weeds, and Simon is expanding our greens and winter crops for extended seasons. Our kitchen, bakery, and cannery keep finding new ways to process our vegetables, fruits, and meats to create more products for our customers to try. A young woman on our staff who has been trained in viticulture has planted our first vineyard. The grapes will be used for jams and fresh eating.

On an island it is easier to conceive of finite-ness. In America at large the experience has been that there are no limits: go west, go up, get more. Here on the Island each resource is limited. The natural resources of the Island—good fishing and hunting, shellfishing, crop fields and pastures, and nature trails on conservation land—help us share our values with each other, reinforcing the bond between Islanders. This environment is supportive to farmers trying to earn a part or all of their living by selling local food.

Our Island values have helped the Vineyard become a prime place for people who want to keep land free for farms and for conservation. Here, we want to eat flavorful fresh eggs, grass-fed, hormone-free beef, humanely raised chicken, fresh vegetables, and even milk and cheese from cows and goats raised here. Here, we also want to teach our children about what that means.

It is gratifying to see bright young people eager to learn agriculture and to witness the evolution of respect and demand for wholesome, fresh, sustainably-grown food. I hope they'll become the next generation of farmers and locavores. And that, just as I did, they will want to protect our land for the many creatures who call Martha's Vineyard home.

ASPARAGUS
An Everlasting Crop

Asparagus is a unique crop, different from all the others at Morning Glory, because it is a perennial. Unlike most other crops that are planted annually from seed, asparagus has only been planted twice at the farm in twenty-two years. The first planting lasted for fourteen years; the current crop was planted in 2005.

The first year after planting, small, wispy shoots come up and are left untouched. In year two, the farmers harvest for just one week, then two the following year, until they can harvest the asparagus for six weeks, from early May to mid or late June.

Asparagus shoots protrude from the ground in the early springtime. They resemble little elves peeking out of the earth, with their straight bodies and purple, petal-like heads bent ever-so-slightly toward the sun.

The edible part of an asparagus plant is the shoot, the very first part to break through the soil. Without all the foliage that usually precedes mature vegetables, a field of asparagus is quite a surprising, slightly shocking sight to see.

"I thought someone was playing a practical joke on me the first time I saw it," said Cammie Taylor, a member of the field crew. "It looks like someone just took an asparagus spear and stuck it back in the soil."

The asparagus grow fast, about a centimeter an hour on hot days. The asparagus can shoot up half their harvest height or more in a single day. Eventually, they start to grow up too fast for the field crew to keep up, and the date for the final harvest is set.

That last harvest is a huge one. Every single spear must be cut, no matter what size. The bounty usually weighs in at around five hundred pounds. The smallest asparagus go to the kitchen, where even the very bottoms that most people snap off and discard are put to use.

Once the final harvest is over, the farmers' work is done, and the plant's work begins. The shoots come up once again, and each purple petal branches out. Every rigid spear transforms into the wild, willowy fern it longs to be. These branches shade out the growth of new weeds, ensuring that the soil's nutrients are taken up by the roots and put toward the plant's progeny. Its foliage absorbs sunlight and makes food for storage.

Morning Glory takes pride in this perennial crop, which is grown as "garden style asparagus," as Simon Athearn explains. Some large-scale asparagus farms plant it annually, which produces really skinny spears. Morning Glory dedicates an acre to the plants for as long as they do well there. As a result, the farm's asparagus is all different sizes, but overall fatter than what you will find in the grocery store.

The wider the girth, the more tender the spear. In a fat asparagus, the ratio of tender part to fibrous part favors the eater. "Fatness is a sign of health," says Simon.

Asparagus Quiche

1 pie crust, uncooked (recipe, page 184)

8 eggs

½ c. sour cream

1 c. milk

1 tsp. smooth Dijon mustard

1 tsp. finely minced fresh herbs: dill, tarragon, chives, etc.

½ c. leeks ragout (recipe, page 14)

1 bunch asparagus, 8–15 stalks (snap or cut off the bottom third, reserve these for stock in the Spring Asparagus Potage)

½ tsp. sea salt

¼ tsp. black pepper

Preheat oven to 375°.

Whisk together eggs, sour cream, and milk in a large bowl.

Spread mustard in the bottom of the pie shell, sprinkle with herbs and spread leeks ragout over herbs. Pour the egg mixture into the pie shell, top with asparagus spears. Sprinkle with salt and pepper.

Bake 25 minutes; rotate the quiche for even cooking. Cook for an additional 15–20 minutes, or until knife comes out clean and the egg is set, not soft or jiggly.

Let stand 5–10 minutes.

CHEF'S NOTE: Asparagus will be at its most flavorful if blanched, roasted, or grilled prior to incorporating into the quiche.

CROP NOTES: *Our asparagus season is rather short, and we find little variation from start to end. The significant variable is the size, both in length and in girth; this variation affects cooking time and technique. We strongly recommend that you not pass over the thick stalks for the pencil-thin ones. The thick stalks are incredibly flavorful and wonderfully moist. They will require peeling for the middle third of the stalk; the thin ones need only to be snapped at the breaking point.*

Leeks Ragout

2 Tbsp. butter

2 Tbsp. extra virgin olive oil

2 medium white onions, medium dice

4 celery ribs, medium dice

2 leeks, medium dice

½ bulb of fennel, cored and medium dice

2 Tbsp. herbs, finely minced: thyme, tarragon, parsley, chives

1 tsp. sea salt

½ tsp. pepper

¼ tsp. nutmeg

¼ tsp. celery seed

In large skillet, melt butter with olive oil over medium-high heat. Add all ingredients.

Cook 15 minutes, covered, stirring occasionally, allowing the vegetables to steam; this allows the vegetables to release moisture and sugars without caramelizing and browning.

Uncover and cook 15 minutes, until vegetables are soft and translucent.

Turn out of skillet, let cool, and set aside.

CHEF'S NOTE: This is a standard item used throughout our cooking. We make it ahead in large batches: then we use it as a layer in our quiches, bean and vegetable salads, other egg dishes, toppings for foccacia, and even on pasta. This will keep for 7 to 10 days when properly refrigerated.

CROP NOTES: *These core vegetables are available to use for most of the year. We tend to use mature crops in recipes such as this.*

Baked Eggs with Leeks, Spinach, and Asparagus

3 Tbsp. unsalted butter

1 large leek, washed and thinly sliced into half moons

¼ c. raw, unfiltered apple cider vinegar

¼ c. milk

Pinch of nutmeg

8 oz. baby spinach leaves

Salt and pepper to taste

6 eggs

18 spears asparagus

1 Tbsp. fresh chives, finely chopped

Hot sauce (optional)

Recipe contributed by Joan Chaput of West Tisbury

Preheat oven to 300°.

Melt the butter in a large cast-iron skillet. Add the leeks and sauté on low heat until tender and sweet, about 10 minutes. Add vinegar, milk, and nutmeg. Bring to a simmer, stir in spinach, and cook until wilted.

Season with salt and pepper.

Using the back of a large spoon, create 6 small wells. Crack an egg into each well.

Put pan in oven, bake 8–10 minutes, or until egg whites are opaque and the yolks are almost firm.

Meanwhile, steam the asparagus.

Place asparagus on individual plates and top with egg and spinach mixture.

Garnish with chives and hot sauce.

CROP NOTES: Spinach: *Early-season spinach, available during asparagus season, is naturally tenderer; remove the stems prior to washing. If using thick-stalk asparagus, peel above the natural break.*

Asparagus and Spring Onion Potage

SOUP

2 bunches asparagus

2 Tbsp. butter

2 Tbsp. plus 1 tsp. extra virgin
    olive oil

2 ribs celery, diced. Save

trimmings for stock

½ lb. spring onion bulbs, about
    8, coarsely chopped. Save
    trimmings for stock

1 leek, coarsely chopped. Save
    trimmings for stock

1 tsp. nutmeg

¼ tsp. cayenne pepper

1 tsp. sea salt

¼ tsp. black pepper

1 Tbsp. sherry vinegar

2 lb. new white potatoes, quartered

2 qts. asparagus-vegetable stock

1 Tbsp. fresh tarragon, chopped

¼ tsp. lemon zest

Remove top 1 inch of asparagus tips, set aside. Take the next 3 inches of asparagus and coarsely chop. Save trimmings for stock.

In 6-qt. pot, melt butter and 2 tbsp. olive oil together over medium heat. Add celery, onion, and leeks; sauté 8–10 minutes. Add nutmeg, cayenne pepper, salt, black pepper, and sherry vinegar; toss. Add potatoes and stock, bring to a boil, add chopped asparagus; simmer and cook until potatoes are soft.

Blend in blender, or use an immersion blender, until smooth.

Stir in tarragon and lemon zest.

While the soup is cooking, toss the asparagus tips with 1 tsp. olive oil. Lightly toast or sauté and set aside for garnish.

CHEF'S NOTE: A potage is a category of thick soups, stews, or porridges, in some of which meat and vegetables are boiled together with water until they form into a thick mush. Since it does not need flour, it is gluten free.

STOCK

2 qts. cold water

Trimmings from soup preparation

Preheat oven to 300°.

Place the asparagus ends and the trimmings from the celery, onions, and leeks in a roasting pan. Roast 12–15 minutes, or until just beginning to brown.

In sauce pot, add water and roasted trimmings, bring to a boil.

Reduce heat, and simmer 30–35 minutes.

Strain and serve hot.

CROP NOTES: Asparagus: *This is a great location for large or mid-sized stalks.* **Potatoes:** *Our new potatoes do not need to be peeled prior to cooking. The skins add wonderful flavor and fall apart.*

Spring Asparagus Smoothie

1 cucumber, coarsely chopped, skin on if fresh, remove if waxed

½ lb. asparagus, coarsely chopped, bottom section removed

¼ lb. young cabbage, kale, or chard, stems removed

½ c. strawberries, hulled

Place all ingredients in blender. Begin at low speed, increase speed as the fruit and vegetables begin to liquefy. (If large pieces impede proper functioning, turn off blender, and with rubber spatula, mix up contents.) Blend for 2 minutes. Consume fresh or refrigerate up to two days.

Note: If refrigerating, simply shake the smoothie well before enjoying.

CROP NOTES: Asparagus: *Another great use for off-sized stalks; the woody bottom should not be used here.* **Strawberries:** *Ripe, even bruised, fruit is perfect for smoothies.* **Spring offerings:** *Any complementary early crop is desirable for both texture (water content) and flavor.*

Fish Tacos with Roasted Asparagus

Canola or Olive oil cooking spray

1 egg

1 c. whole-wheat bread crumbs

¼ c. walnuts, ground

1 lb. white fish fillets—sole, cod, haddock, flounder, etc.

2 lb. asparagus, thick ends removed

1 c. peach, diced

1 c. cherry tomatoes, halved

¼ c. cilantro, chopped

¼ tsp. sea salt

1 lime, juiced

8 small corn tortillas or 4 medium whole-wheat flour tortillas

1 c. red cabbage, thinly sliced

1 c. red bell pepper, thinly sliced

½ c. part-skim mozzarella cheese, shredded (optional)

Recipe contributed by Vineyard Nutrition

Heat oven to 400°.

Spray 2 baking sheets with oil; canola for fish, olive for asparagus.

Whisk egg in a bowl.

Mix together bread crumbs and ground walnuts in a large plate.

Dip fish fillets in egg, coat with crumbs, and lay on baking sheet.

Layer asparagus in single layer on olive oil baking sheet.

Roast both sheets for 15–20 minutes, depending on thickness of fish (check fish, turn asparagus after 10 minutes).

In a small bowl, mix peaches, cherry tomatoes, cilantro, salt, and lime juice.

2 to 3 minutes before fish and asparagus are done, put tortillas in oven to warm.

Layer 2 corn tortillas or 1 whole-wheat tortilla per person with ¼ of the fish; top each serving with cabbage, pepper, cheese, and ¼ of the peach salsa.

Serve with generous portion of asparagus.

Quick-Braised Asparagus
with Dijon-Herb Pan Sauce

SPECIAL EQUIPMENT: 10-INCH STRAIGHT-SIDED SAUTÉ PAN WITH LID / SERVINGS: 3 AS A SIDE DISH

2 tsp. lemon juice

1 ½ tsp. maple syrup

½ tsp. Dijon mustard

1 Tbsp. extra virgin olive oil

1 Tbsp. unsalted butter

1 bunch asparagus, medium-thick, each spear trimmed to 6 inches in length

¼ tsp. kosher salt

¼ c. low-sodium chicken broth

1 tsp. fresh chervil or thyme, roughly chopped

Recipe contributed by Susie Middleton, cookbook author and West Tisbury farmer. "This is one of my very favorite preparations for fresh, local, big meaty spears of asparagus. There's a depth of flavor here from the browning, yet the dish only takes about 15 minutes, start to finish." Susie's newest cookbook is called Fresh from the Farm.

Combine the lemon juice, maple syrup, and mustard in a small bowl.

In sauté pan, heat the olive oil and ½ Tbsp. butter over medium-high heat. When the butter has melted and is bubbling, add the asparagus and salt; toss well to coat. Arrange in one layer and cook, without stirring, until the undersides are nicely browned, 4–5 minutes.

Using tongs, turn each spear over and cook, without stirring, just until the other side is beginning to brown, about 2 minutes. Carefully pour the chicken broth into the pan and immediately cover it. Simmer until the liquid reduces almost completely; 1 or 2 tsp. will be left, about 2 minutes.

Uncover, take the pan off the heat, add the remaining butter, the lemon mixture, and most of the herbs. Stir gently with a silicone spatula, incorporating any browned bits from the bottom, until the butter has melted and the pan sauce is slightly glazy.

Transfer the asparagus to a serving platter or plates and pour the pan sauce over it, scraping all the sauce out of the pan.

Garnish with remaining herbs.

Roasted Asparagus

1 bunch asparagus, "snapped" washed, and thoroughly dried

3 Tbsp. extra virgin olive oil

½ tsp. sea salt—coarse

1 leek (white only) cut lengthwise, then across at ¼ inch

½ tsp. coarse or country mustard

1 tsp. raw, unfiltered apple cider vinegar

4 oz. pea shoots

1 tsp. chives—finely minced

3–4 turns black pepper mill

Preheat oven to 425°.

Line roasting pan with parchment paper (optional). Layer the asparagus across the pan, drizzle with olive oil, and sprinkle the salt. Bake for 12–15 minutes or until the spears begin to caramelize (brown).

Remove from oven and pour off excess oil and liquid into a sauté pan. Place over medium-high heat and add the leeks. Sauté for 5–6 minutes or until the leeks soften but do not turn color. Stir in the mustard and vinegar. Increase heat to high and add the shoots. Toss thoroughly and remove from heat. Add the chives and pepper.

Place the asparagus on a serving platter and spoon the pea-shoot mixture on top.

> **CHEF'S NOTE:** Tender pea shoots need only a moment of heat to release their flavor. If longer than 3–4 inches, the more mature plant may be a bit stringy; simply cut across in 3" sections.

CROP NOTES: *Thick-stalk asparagus works well with this technique, yet will require a bit more roasting time than the popular pencil thin spears. Peeling the ends of the asparagus is not a necessary step for roasting. Peeled stalks may become dry as a result of the roasting process. Wintered leeks (left in the ground throughout the season) are a naturally sweet accompaniment; early spring or green onions would be a great substitute. Likewise, chives are ready to trim during the asparagus harvest.*

CORN
The Crop That Truly Defines Morning Glory

*Jim Athearn begins planning his corn crop months before planting starts in May. He sits down at his desk, beneath a bookcase with titles that reveal his life as a farmer—*Weeds of the North Central States, Growing for Market. *In one productive afternoon, with a pencil and a spiral-bound notebook, he plans a season of corn: thirty plantings, give or take, of a dozen varieties.*

Jim's goal is that a "block" of corn, a field planted with one single variety, will ripen every two to three days over the course of three months, so that there is never a lull, nor a glut in supply.

"It's just simple arithmetic," Jim says. But his notebooks of years past show that it takes more than math. This is farming, and there are always elements of the unknown: the weather, the experiments in planting methods, the birds, the raccoons. The Athearns only want to stock *fresh* corn at the stand, even if it means that for a day or two they have to sell off-Island corn to give their own the time it needs to mature on the stalk.

There is an old saying about sweet corn that speaks to its quick deterioration after harvest: get the water boiling, and then go pick the corn. New varieties of corn have made the adage obsolete, because they can maintain their sugars for three days or more. Despite the advances in modern varieties that store longer**,** Morning Glory stays true to its motto, "Never sold a day old."

Picking only the ripest ears of corn takes training. Out in the fields, Simon and Dan Athearn and their corn team walk through the rows at a measured pace. With one hand, they hold up a bushel bag, while the other hand is free to harvest the corn. Every ear is hand-selected. The corn pickers have trained their senses to recognize the signs of an ear at peak ripeness, an ear that meets the Morning Glory standards. If it makes the cut, a slight twist and downward tug separates the ear from the stalk, and it gets tossed into the bag.

"You can see *some* things," said Simon, like the color of the silk and the size of the ear. Dark, matted silks mean it is ripe, but completely dried-out silks could be overripe. Some ears are clearly too small, and others have been ravaged by raccoons. Those are left on the stalk.

Other factors need to be felt for. And finally, how does it taste? Generally, Morning Glory's corn is sweet and the kernels are tender. They should practically burst under the slightest pressure of your teeth. The pickers are encouraged to taste the corn out in the field, in keeping to a Morning Glory motto: *When in doubt, eat it.*

FIGHTING THOSE WORMS

"It is not polite to peel/strip the corn"
—SIGN POSTED JUST ABOVE THE CORN COUNTER

The sign is not an excuse for hiding worms. It's just how the Athearns feel. Stripping the corn inside makes a mess, and who wants to buy an ear already stripped and rejected?

It's not easy, growing worm-free corn on Martha's Vineyard. Research has shown that earworm pressure on the Island is four times what it is further inland. For several years, as he got started on the farm, Jim grew corn organically. Each time, the corn was too wormy to be salable.

These days, Jim and Simon spray the corn with pesticides when they feel it is needed. Jim loves corn, and he knows it will never be fresher or tastier than when it's grown locally. He follows the laws of pesticide usage, and he trusts the agency that tests for safety.

"Why deprive myself of putting a particular tool in my tool box that might be used only once a year, but when I need it, I really need it?" said Jim.

Corn and Mushroom Risotto

12 oz. mushrooms, halved or quartered; reserve stems

2 ears corn, kernelled; reserve cobs

2 Tbsp. extra virgin olive oil

½ tsp. sea salt

1 Tbsp. butter

1 Tbsp. extra virgin olive oil

1 medium onion, small dice; reserve skins

1 leek, medium dice; reserve greens

¼ tsp. nutmeg

1 tsp. sea salt

¼ tsp. black pepper

1 Tbsp. sage, finely minced

1 c. Arborio rice

1 qt. Corn Broth (recipe, page 26)

¼ c. grated cheese, parmesan or substitute a local New England hard grating cheese

Preheat oven to 375°.

Mix together mushrooms, corn, oil and salt. Place on lined baking sheet. Bake 20–22 minutes, until mushrooms are soft, but not dry or crisp, and corn is just beginning to caramelize. The corn will be spotty tan.

While mushrooms and corn are roasting, melt butter and olive oil in saucepan over medium-high heat. Add onions, leeks, nutmeg, salt, pepper, and sage; mix. Stir occasionally until onions are soft and translucent, 8–10 minutes.

Lower heat to medium-low, stir in rice; mix until coated with oil. Stirring constantly, add broth 1 cup at a time, adding more broth when the rice has absorbed the previous cup. Continue adding broth until all has been absorbed. Fold in mushrooms, corn, and cheese.

Serve warm.

> **CHEF'S NOTE:** The complementary vegetables are all at the height of their season along with the corn. Any variety of onion will be fine. Forgo canned broth for the simple corn broth. The flavor of the vegetables during season will be worth the extra time.

CROP NOTES: Corn: *Larger kernelled, more robust flavored corn varieties, such as Providence, are perfect in the risotto.*

Corn Chowder

4 ears corn, kernelled; reserve cobs

1 lb. onions, 2 medium, medium dice; reserve skins

2 ribs celery, medium dice; reserve ends and leaves

1 leek, white only, medium dice; reserve green

2 lb. Yukon gold potatoes, divided, 1 lb. large dice, 1 lb. medium dice

1 c. milk or cream

¼ lb. pork belly, salt pork or bacon, medium dice, or cut in strips

2 cloves garlic, finely minced

¼ tsp. mustard seed or ½ tsp. Dijon mustard

¼ tsp. crushed red pepper

½ tsp. thyme, finely minced

Sea salt

Black pepper

1 tsp. dill, coarsely chopped

¼ tsp. lemon zest

Corn broth

Preheat oven to 400°.

Prepare corn broth (see chef's note below.)

Place large diced potatoes in 4-qt. saucepan with enough broth to cover, boil over medium-high heat, reduce heat to medium, cook 20 minutes. Strain, return potatoes to pot, add milk, and stir vigorously to combine texture of mashed potatoes.

Over medium heat, render pork in 6-qt. saucepan. When fat is opaque and begins to brown, add onion, celery, and leek; cook 8 minutes. Add garlic, mustard seed, red pepper, thyme, salt, and pepper. Continue cooking while adding corn kernels and medium diced potatoes. Cover with 2 qts. of reserved broth, boil, and simmer 30 minutes.

Fold in mashed potatoes; mix until combined. Add salt and pepper to taste. Sprinkle dill and lemon zest over soup prior to serving. Keep extra broth in the refrigerator and use in dishes that call for water or canned vegetable broths.

> **CHEF'S NOTE:** Corn broth is a great way to use leftover parts of plants. Combine cobs, onion skins, and leek greens, roast until beginning to brown, 18–20 minutes. In 6 qt. sauce pan over medium-high heat, combine 3 qts. water, roasted trimmings, bay leaf and any stems and herb ends, boil. Reduce heat to medium, cook 30 minutes, strain and set aside. Keep broth in the fridge and use in dishes that call for water or canned vegetable broth.

Warm Corn Salad and Hot Italian Sausage

1 lb. farm hot Italian sausage, removed from casing

2 Tbsp. extra virgin olive oil

1 lb. small to medium Cremini mushrooms, stemmed and quartered

1 tsp. rosemary, finely chopped

¼ tsp. fennel seed

¼ tsp. mustard seed

4 scallions, whites diced, greens cut in ½″ slices

2 ribs celery, cut in ½″ slices

4 cobs corn, kernelled

1 Tbsp. dill, coarsely chopped

¼ tsp. sea salt

⅛ tsp. black pepper

This recipe can be doubled and tripled easily, to serve just you or hordes.

Preheat oven to 400°.

Place sausage on a lined roasting pan, bake for 15–18 minutes.

Meanwhile, heat skillet and oil over medium-high heat, add mushrooms. Sauté 6 minutes; add rosemary, fennel and mustard seeds, scallion whites and celery; cook 5 minutes.

Gently stir in corn and scallion greens; cook 2 minutes. Place in a serving platter; slice sausage and place over the corn. Drizzle the remaining juices from the roasting pan over the salad. Garnish with the dill.

Salt and pepper to taste.

Summer Corn-off-the-Cob Sauté
with Garlic, Ginger, and Fresh Herbs

1 Tbsp. plus 1 tsp. unsalted butter

1 Tbsp. extra virgin olive oil

1½ c. sweet, yellow onion, diced small (1 medium-large onion)

Kosher salt

2 c. corn kernels, 4 ears

1 Tbsp. fresh ginger, finely chopped

1 heaping tsp. fresh garlic, minced

1 tsp. freshly grated lime zest

Fresh ground black pepper

¼ lime

3 Tbsp. fresh tender herbs, chopped (basil, parsley and chives, or cilantro and mint)

Recipe contributed by Susie Middleton, cookbook author and West Tisbury farmer: "Don't worry when you see a lot of brown stuff building up on the bottom of the pan. When you sauté corn, it always releases a bit of starch, which causes the browning. The brown stuff tastes really good though, so I incorporate a couple of ways to get it back into the sauté. First, I suggest you let the sauté sit for a few minutes in the pan after cooking. As the vegetables rest, they (especially the onions) will release some moisture that will loosen some of the brown bits, and can be stirred in. Second, after the lime is squeezed in, the added moisture will loosen more. A wooden spoon works best for this."

In skillet, melt 1 Tbsp. butter and the oil over medium-low heat. Add onions and ½ tsp. salt, cover and cook, stirring occasionally, until translucent, 5 minutes. Uncover, turn the heat up to medium, and sauté, stirring frequently, until lightly browned, 4–5 minutes.

Add remaining butter, corn, and ½ tsp. salt. Cook, stirring frequently and scraping the bottom of the pan with a wooden spoon, until the corn is tender but still slightly toothy to the bite, 4–5 minutes. The corn will begin to intensify in color, glisten, and be somewhat shrunken in size.

Add the ginger and garlic, cook, stirring, until very fragrant, 30 seconds to 1 minute. Stir in lime zest and remove pan from heat. Let sit 2–3 minutes, stir again to loosen more browned starch from the bottom of the pan.

Season the sauté with a few generous grinds of black pepper and a good squeeze of lime. Stir in half the herbs. Let sit 3 more minutes.

Stir and season to taste with salt, pepper, and lime juice. Stir in remaining herbs just before serving.

Tip from Susie: "I find the safest way to cut corn off the cob is to snap the shucked ears in half first. This takes a little elbow grease, but it works fine. Put one half, cut side down, on a large cutting board and slice down the cob with a sharp knife using a sawing motion. Keep turning the cob until you've cut off all the kernels. Repeat with the other half. For convenience, I also put a large (old) dishtowel over my cutting board before I start. When I'm done cutting, I can fold the corners of the towel up and easily transfer the kernels to a bowl. Any way you do it, be aware that corn kernels do have a tendency to go flying when you cut them."

Corn Bread

½ c. butter, melted, cooled

1 c. evaporated cane juice, or ¾ c. granulated sugar

2 eggs

1¼ c. whole milk

⅔ c. sour cream

2 Tbsp. unsulfured molasses

1½ c. corn kernels, 2 medium ears

1½ c. coarse cornmeal

2 c. all-purpose flour

½ c. whole-wheat flour

2 Tbsp. baking powder

1 tsp. sea salt

Non-stick spray for pans

Preheat oven to 350°.

In stand mixer fitted with paddle attachment, combine butter and sugar; mix at medium speed for 2 minutes. Switch to medium-low speed; add eggs one at a time. Pour in milk, sour cream, and molasses. Switch to low speed, add corn kernels, and mix until just combined. Pour wet mixture into a separate bowl.

In clean mixer bowl with paddle, combine corn meal, flours, baking powder, and salt, mix thoroughly. Reintroduce the wet mixture into the dry and beat at medium speed for 2 minutes.

Lightly spray pans or line muffin tins. Pour in batter, bake 25 minutes, spin pan, bake 22 more minutes or until a thin knife comes out clean. Remove from oven.

Loaf pans should rest 5 minutes. Then remove bread from pans and place on cooling rack. Muffins can be removed immediately to a cooling rack.

Roasted Corn, Sweet Onion, and Herb Polenta

ROASTED CORN

1½–2 c. corn kernels, about 2 ears

¼ tsp. sea salt

¼ tsp. smoked paprika

¼ tsp. cumin

Pinch of black pepper

1 Tbsp. olive oil

POLENTA

1 Tbsp. butter

1 Tbsp. extra virgin olive oil

½ lb. sweet onions, about 3 small, or 2 medium onions, cut in half and finely sliced

½ tsp. sea salt

⅛ tsp. black pepper

1 Tbsp. mixed herbs: thyme, rosemary, and summer savory

1 c. coarse cornmeal

4 c. commercial or homemade vegetable stock or water

Preheat oven to 350°.

Combine all roasted corn ingredients and spread out on a parchment lined baking sheet.

Roast 10–12 minutes until corn begins to caramelize; corn will begin to turn a medium brown. Remove from oven and set aside.

In a 6-qt. pot, melt butter and olive oil over medium-high heat. Add onions, salt, pepper, and herbs; cook 8–10 minutes until onions are soft.

Whisk in cornmeal, and whisk until fully coated with hot oil mixture.

Slowly whisk in stock, continuing to whisk over medium heat until smooth.

Bring to a boil, reduce heat to low, and cook for 18–20 minutes until thoroughly smooth, stirring regularly.

Fold in roasted corn.

Alternative 1: Bleu Cheese and Spinach
In place of corn, fold in ¼ lb. crumbled bleu cheese (we're fans of Great Hill Blue in Marion) and 1 cup clean, coarsely chopped fresh spinach leaves into hot polenta. Let stand 5 minutes and serve.

Alternative 2: Mushroom and Farm Leek
Add ½ lb. chopped mushrooms and 2 diced leeks to onions and herbs. Continue to cook according to directions. Let sit up to 5 minutes and serve.

CROP NOTES: Corn: *Roasting the corn before introducing it to the polenta requires a full-flavored corn with a medium to large kernel. We recommend our popular varieties Providence or Cameo.* **Onion:** *Fresh or uncured varieties offer a sweeter, more subtle flavor, an appropriate match to the corn. Traditional cured onions will have a stronger, more pronounced flavor.* **Herbs:** *A great location for summer savory. Substitute rosemary or thyme.*

FARM MEATS

Chickens and Pigs and Cows, Oh My

Braised Beef Shank or Crosscut Shank

2 beef shanks

2 qts. Basic Meat Brine (recipe, page 39)

Salt

Pepper

1 Tbsp. canola oil

1 lb. carrots, 4 large, coarsely chopped

4 ribs celery, coarsely chopped

1 lb. onions, 4 small, halved or medium cut in quarters

1 leek, white only, coarsely chopped

3 lb. tomatoes, about 8, cut in 8ths, or 16ths if large

1 Tbsp. extra virgin olive oil

1 Tbsp. fennel seed

½ tsp. red chili flakes

1 Tbsp. winter savory, (1 sprig)

1 lemon, meat only, cut in 8ths (Note: this is a great way to use zested lemons; cut away the rest of the skin and core membranes)

2 qts. beef broth, or more as necessary

Flat leaf parsley, coarsely chopped

Place shanks in large lidded container; add brine to cover. Cover and refrigerate overnight, about 12 hours. When ready to use, drain and pat dry; season with salt and pepper.

Heat oil in heavy bottom skillet over medium-high heat. Sear each shank individually until it is a dark brown and uniformly seared on both sides. Remove and set aside.

Preheat oven to 350°.

Combine all vegetables, olive oil, seasonings, herbs, and lemon; thoroughly mix and place in roasting pan. Nestle in shanks, cover with broth, cover and bake for 3 hours. It may be necessary to add water or more broth to the pan if the vegetables are fully exposed and appear to be roasting.

Roast for a total of 3 ½ to 4 hours, or until the meat begins to fall off the bone.

Let cool for 10 minutes before handling. Place the shank over risotto rice; ladle some of the braised vegetable mixture over the shank. Ladle the remaining braised vegetables and liquid into blender (or bowl if using an immersion blender); puree. Ladle this sauce over the dish and garnish with flat leaf parsley.

> **CHEF'S NOTE:** This is great served over risotto or with a grained salad.

BEEF: A THOUSAND POUNDS OF GRASS-FED DELICIOUSNESS

The nosy cattle, a motley herd of Hereford, Black Angus, and Limousins, stand in a pack and stare at Dan Athearn, who is in charge of Morning Glory's cattle division.

Dan walks the width of the pasture, gathering wooden posts and rolling up the fence that connects them. He moves back twenty feet or so, replants the posts, rolls out the wire fence, and turns on the electricity. The difference, to the cattle, is a new strip of land with lush, green grasses.

"Instead of feeding them grain, you just use such a simple infrastructure to feed your cows," says Dan, referencing the low-tech fence. "In a way, the electric fence replaces the combine," a machine for harvesting, threshing, and cleaning grains, which feed much of the livestock in America.

This quotidian routine of moving cattle to new pasture is called strip-grazing. They get a daily helping of fresh grass and move on to new pasture the next day. When they are moved off a piece of pasture, the grasses grow back quickly, so the herd can graze there again.

Speckled with large boulders, the land at Bethaven Farm in West Tisbury, where Dan grazes most of the herd, prohibits tractor work. Dan uses the herd to clear the land of large weeds and brush by throwing hay on top of the undesirable growth. The cattle go after the hay, trampling the weeds, and spreading seeds contained within the hay grasses. In the springtime, the rocky land that was thick with weeds and brush grows back as pasture. The cattle did the work to transform it.

Basic Meat Brine

SPECIAL EQUIPMENT: LARGE, NONREACTIVE CONTAINER WITH LID / YIELD: 1 GALLON

1 c. seasonal fruits or their nectar/ juice; peaches, pears, apples

3 qts. cool water

2 c. raw, unfiltered apple cider vinegar or white vinegar

2 Tbsp. seeds, any combination of coriander, caraway, mustard, and dill

1 tsp. dried red chili flakes

1 Tbsp. black peppercorns

3–4 sprigs fresh herbs—rosemary, savory, or thyme

½ c. salt, dissolved in 1 c. warm water

2–3 Tbsp. sugar, if omitting the fruit

Coarsely chop or mash the fruit and place in nonreactive container. Add the remaining ingredients and stir to combine. Best if made a day in advance.

Brine can be kept in the refrigerator without the fresh herbs for an extended period of time. Simply remove herbs prior to refrigerating.

Use
3 qts. for one 4–5 lb. picnic ham
1–2 qts. for one roast
1 qt. for 1 lb. shanks
1 cup for one 8 oz. pork chop

CHEF'S NOTE: We brine all of the Morning Glory meat we use in the kitchen: chicken, pork, and beef. The animals raised on the farm move around more than most conventionally raised animals. That means they have more muscle and less fat. Brining helps to clean the meat and leads to increased moisture and tenderness. It also reduces cooking time and weight loss of meat during cooking. Brining seasons the meat throughout, as the salt is absorbed into the meat over time, rather than seasoning just the surface right before cooking.

CROP NOTES: Peaches: *Ripe, even bruised peaches are a perfect natural source of sugar and add a wonderful layer of flavor. Sometimes, Morning Glory sells "imperfect peaches" at a reduced price. These are peaches that may not look perfect or have a small bruise that should be cut out. They are great for baking or cooking, but they could also be sliced and frozen, and eaten during the winter—still delicious, still local.*

Molasses Chicken, Apple, and Leeks

¼ c. molasses

¼ c. mustard

¼ c. raw, unfiltered apple cider vinegar

¾ c. apple cider

4 split breasts on the bone, or 4 statler breasts, first wing bone attached

2 medium apples, peeled,

2 large leeks, 4 small, white only, sliced in ½″ rounds

2 sprigs fresh savory, thyme, or anise hyssop

Sea salt

Black pepper

Preheat oven to 375°.

Whisk together molasses, mustard, apple cider vinegar, and apple cider. Add chicken; toss to coat. Set aside 15 minutes.

Peel and core apples, and cut into ½-inch slices.

In baking dish, layer apples, leeks, and savory, or other herb choice. Place chicken on top; pour remainder of marinade over the chicken. Season with salt and pepper. Bake 55 minutes; baste after 30 minutes and again every 10–12 minutes. Baste one final time upon removing from oven.

The molasses glaze will create a dark crust.

Serve with a warm salad, such as Three Grains, Three Greens (recipe, page 62).

> **CHEF'S NOTE:** We do not recommend the use of boneless skinless breasts for this recipe. The chicken will be dry. A whole bird, cut into quarters, will be fine as well, and the leg-thigh section may take 10–12 minutes longer in the oven. Using a statler breast—a boneless chicken breast with the small wing bone left intact and skin still on—provides great taste and an easier to eat portion.

GARLIC AND THOSE LUSCIOUS SCAPES

Morning Glory grows hardneck varieties of garlic, so called because the stem that starts between the cloves and protrudes from the ground is stiff. Hardneck garlic also has fewer, but larger, cloves of garlic, requiring less peeling in the kitchen.

Although garlic is not available until late July or early August, you can find garlic scapes in the stand in the late spring, and green garlic beginning in early summer (green because the leaves are still green at the time of harvest; without a dried, outer skin, green garlic has a shorter shelf-life).

Scapes are mellower than cloves of garlic, slightly sweet, and have a soft, meaty texture when cooked that enables them to be the star of a dish, as well as a seasoning agent. Sauté them, roast them, grill them. Keep them whole, chop them, mince them, or process them. In the Morning Glory kitchen, the scapes are roasted and processed with oil and vinegar to become a flavorful, zesty dressing. Simon Athearn caramelizes them just like onions.

Salt-Crusted Pork Chops

SPECIAL EQUIPMENT: LARGE, CAST-IRON SKILLET / SERVINGS: 6–8

1 pt. Basic Meat Brine
(recipe, page 39)

6–8 pork chops, 1″ thick

Sea salt

Black pepper

¼ c. canola oil

Preheat oven to 400°.

Place chops and brine in sealable bag or in nonreactive bowl; let rest 1 hour, remove chops, and pat dry. Season both sides of chops with salt and pepper.

Heat oil in skillet over medium–high heat. Lay chops flat in skillet; cook in batches if necessary. There should be a strong sizzling sound when the chops hit the skillet. Sear 3 minutes, turn chops over, sear 3 additional minutes. Place skillet, if all chops fit, or place chops in roasting pan, in oven; bake 8 minutes, until internal temperature reads 130°.

Remove pork from oven. Let rest 10 minutes before serving to redistribute juices. Serve with Warm Eggplant and Tomato Salad (recipe, page 187) ladled on top.

CHICKENS AND THEIR "MANSION"

Near Jim and Debbie Athearn's home, four cows and seven hundred chickens share an acre of dedicated pasture. May through November, the chickens live in homemade mobile units called chicken tractors, and every day Jim moves the birds to a new strip of land where they feed off fresh grass. Their job is twofold: to eat, and to fertilize.

The cows get the first helping of pasture, and as they move along strip by strip, the chickens follow and eat what remains of the grasses, as well as bugs for extra protein. While there, the chickens help fertilize the pasture so that grasses will grow back lush, and the cows and chickens can continue to cycle through. In the springtime, "You can see the strips of green where the chickens went," says Dan Athearn.

Every two weeks, seventy-five chickens are slaughtered on-farm in the Island's Mobile Poultry Processing Trailer, a project instituted by a local nonprofit organization, Island Grown Initiative (IGI). Taz Armstrong, the IGI poultry program coordinator, oversees the chicken processing and has been working with the unit for five years. He was also a two-year Morning Glory field crew member. Chickens are available fresh for four days after the processing, and are then frozen and sold.

Behind Jim and Debbie's house is also the henhouse, nicknamed the "Chicken Mansion," where about eight hundred chickens lay up to sixty dozen eggs a day.

In the wintertime, a self-service refrigerator outside of the stand is stocked with eggs when extras are available. This farm stand system of trust is common on the Island.

Chicken Breasts with Braised Grapes

SPECIAL EQUIPMENT: HEAVY-BOTTOM SKILLET, CASSEROLE DISH / SERVINGS: 4

2 Tbsp. butter

2 Tbsp. olive oil

2 leeks, white only, cut in ¼″ rounds

4 ribs celery, cut in ¼″ slices

½ tsp. celery seed

½ tsp. caraway seed

1 tsp. sea salt

¼ tsp. black pepper

¼ tsp. smoked paprika

¼ tsp. cumin

¼ tsp. cinnamon

½ tsp. thyme, finely chopped

¼ tsp. lemon zest

4 chicken breasts, skin on, wing bone attached

1 bulb fennel, halved, cored, finely julienned

¼ lb. grapes

1 chili pepper, finely diced

1 sprig rosemary

1 qt. chicken stock

Preheat oven to 350°.

In heavy bottom skillet, melt butter and oil over medium heat. Add vegetables, and celery and caraway seeds; cook 10–12 minutes, until soft, but not browned. Remove vegetables from pan and set aside.

Meanwhile, in small bowl, mix together sea salt, pepper, paprika, cumin, cinnamon, thyme, and lemon zest. Season chicken breasts.

Return pan to burner. Increase heat to medium-high. Sear the chicken breasts, skin side down, until golden brown. Turn over and cook 5 minutes. Remove from pan and set aside.

In casserole dish or skillet, if oven proof, line with half the reserved vegetable mixture; top with fennel, grapes, chili pepper, and rosemary. Nestle in chicken breasts, skin side up. Top with remaining vegetable mixture. Pour in enough stock to cover chicken breasts halfway. Cover with foil; bake 40 minutes. Uncover and finish cooking, 15–30 minutes.

Remove from oven and serve chicken over polenta or rice. Ladle grape and vegetable mixture over breasts.

CHEF'S NOTE: 24–48 hours after chicken processing day, we break down a number of birds with the intent of filling the prepared foods stock with rilettes, stock, and liver mousse. We begin by separating thighs, legs, and breasts (off the bone with the first wing segment attached.) The remaining back and rib bones should be reserved for stock.

Sweet and Sour Country-Style Pork Ribs

1 lb. country-style ribs

1 qt. Basic Meat Brine
(recipe, page 39)

1 lb. tomatoes, skin and intact,
½" dice

1 Tbsp. honey

½ lb. slab bacon, cut into ½" cubes

2 Tbsp. Roasted Garlic, 6 cloves
(recipe, page 51)

½ c. raw, unfiltered apple cider
vinegar

1 c. apple cider

½ tsp. lemon zest

½ tsp. dried chili flakes

Salt and pepper

Serve with Country-Style Beans (recipe, page 106)

Place ribs and brine in a zip lock bag. Seal and refrigerate for from four hours to overnight.

Remove from refrigerator, pat dry, and let rest at room temperature for 15–20 minutes. Sprinkle with salt and pepper.

Preheat oven to 250°.

Bring skillet to medium high temperature. Sear the ribs on the meaty sides and place in roasting pan. Reduce the heat under the skillet to medium low and render the bacon. As bacon softens—8 to 20 minutes—add tomatoes, continuing to coo for eight minutes.

Stir in remaining ingredients, bring to a boil, and reduce to a simmer for 10 minutes. Pour over ribs in roasting pan.

Ribs can be covered with aluminum foil and slowly braised for three hours on their own. Or you can add beans from the Country Style Bean recipe from page 106 and cover and cook with the ribs.

> **CHEF'S NOTE:** We recommend cooking this with the Country Style Beans, recipe, page 106. If you do it that way, pour the beans into the roasting pan, then place the ribs on top. Cover with foil, and continue cooking as instructed.

Sausage and Whole-Wheat Pasta

SPECIAL EQUIPMENT: 6-QT. POT, HEAVY-BOTTOM SKILLET / SERVINGS: 4

3 qts. water

½ tsp. sea salt, plus more to salt pasta water

½ lb. flat whole-wheat noodles, such as pappardelle

3 Tbsp. extra virgin olive oil, divided

½ lb. farm pork sausage, sweet or hot, removed from casing

1 leek, white only, cut across and julienned

½ lb. onion, cured, 1 medium or 2–4 small, peeled, halved and julienned

1 tsp. finely minced oregano

½ tsp. mustard seed

½ tsp. caraway seed

¼ tsp. lemon zest

½ lb. Brussels sprouts, stemmed, sliced across 3–5 slices each

4 oz. komatsuna greens; remove stems and cut across in ½" slices similar to slicing a celery stalk; separate greens, and tear into 2" pieces

½ small head red cabbage

1 c. chicken broth

¼ c. sour cream

¼ tsp. black pepper

In 6-qt. pot, bring water and salt to a boil. Add noodles; stir and cook 7–8 minutes. Strain, toss with 1 Tbsp. olive oil, and set aside.

Meanwhile, over medium heat, brown sausage in skillet, breaking meat up in the pan, cook 7–8 minutes. Remove sausage from pan and set aside; retain any fat in the pan.

Add 2 Tbsp. olive oil to pan and allow to come up to temperature. Add leeks, salt, and onions; cook 8 minutes. Add oregano, mustard and caraway seeds, lemon zest, Brussels sprouts, komatsuna stalks, and cabbage; cook 5–6 minutes. Add stock and sour cream; stir. Let the broth heat and bubble on sides of pan.

In a large bowl, toss together the pasta, sausage, komatsuna greens, black pepper, and sautéed vegetables. Allow the greens to wilt before serving.

CROP NOTES: *During the Brussels sprout harvest, red cabbage and leeks are abundant. The onions will have been dried or cured, yet we will still be harvesting any number of our Asian greens. The komatsuna's flavor offers a mild mustardy bite in the richly flavored leaves. Substitute bok choy or mustard greens for komatsuna greens.*

Brined Beef Brisket

3–4 lb. beef brisket

1 gal. Basic Meat Brine (recipe, page 39) or less

2 Tbsp. canola oil

Salt

Black pepper

1 large onion, coarsely chopped

1 leek, white only, coarsely chopped

2 ribs celery, coarsely chopped

4 carrots, coarsely chopped

1 Tbsp. juniper berries; substitute fennel or caraway seeds

1 sprig rosemary

3 sprigs sage

2 c. raw unfiltered apple cider

½ c. Worcestershire sauce, or tamari

½ c. apple cider

¼ c. unsulfured molasses

3 c. beef stock, substitute chicken stock

Combine brisket and enough brine to cover meat in large container; cover and refrigerate overnight, about 12 hours. Strain beef when ready to prepare and pat dry.

In a heavy-bottom skillet, heat oil over medium-high heat. Season meat with salt and pepper; sear the brisket until uniformly caramelized on both sides.

Preheat oven to 350°.

Combine all ingredients in roasting pan. Nestle brisket in the middle of pan, allowing the liquid level to come up to three-quarters of the brisket. Add or remove liquid as necessary. Cover pan, and place in oven. Cook for 4 hours, or until interior temperature reaches 180° and edges pull away slightly when tugged with tongs. Remove from oven.

When slightly cooled, remove brisket from pan and place on plate to cool. Brisket can be served at this point, but it will be more difficult to slice if not sufficiently cooled. Slice brisket across the grain at a slight angle. Place slices in clean roasting pan and spoon original pan juices over the top; if necessary, skim excess fat from the broth. Place back in oven to bring up to temperature.

Note: Pureeing some or all of the braising vegetables in the broth will thicken the sauce and add another layer of flavor.

> CHEF'S NOTE: Grain-fed or commercial briskets will be larger (from 8 to 12 lb.) and fattier than our grass-fed beef. If using commercial beef, ask for a 4–5 lb. brisket in-store as you will need to trim a considerable amount of fat.

THIS LITTLE PIGGY . . .

Over the years, the Athearns have raised an increasing number of pigs and sold an increasing amount of pork, especially in the form of bacon and sausage.

Piglets are easy to raise, explains Jim, so long as you have a good pen: good for the piglets—with dry places as well as mud, and a clean place to unload their food—and good for the farmer. "You spend a lot of time and worry chasing pigs all over the countryside if you don't have a good pen," says Jim.

The stand sells frozen cuts and preparations of pork, including sausage, bacon, baby back and country-style ribs, pork chops, pork butt, and tenderloin. Pork is also featured in many Morning Glory prepared meals.

Morning Glory Farm pigs have the advantage of getting surplus and waste produce to supplement their grain diet, and the Athearns plant several rows of feed corn alongside their sweet corn to store for winter feedings to the pigs.

Roasted Garlic

1 bulb garlic

Olive oil

Sea salt

Preheat oven to 350°.

Cut top ½″ off of garlic bulb, place on lined baking sheet, drizzle with olive oil, and sprinkle with salt. Roast, covered, 22–25 minutes until interior is soft. When bulb is cool enough to touch, grab bulb and squeeze from the bottom up until cloves pop out of skins.

Excess garlic can be stored in refrigerator covered in olive oil for an extended period of time.

Slow-Roasted Brined Beef Roast

SPECIAL EQUIPMENT: LARGE BOWL OR BUCKET FOR BRINING, LARGE, HEAVY-BOTTOMED SKILLET, ROASTING PAN OR DUTCH OVEN / SERVINGS: 4–6

1 3-lb. hindquarter of beef

1 gal. Basic Meat Brine (recipe, page 39)

1 tsp. sea salt, plus more for seasoning meat

½ tsp. coarse black pepper, plus more for seasoning meat

1 lb. carrots, 5–6 medium, cut into 1 ¼-inch pieces

6 medium spring onions, tops removed 4–6 inches from base, stem end removed and remainder cut in half, lengthwise

2 leeks, cut into 1″ rounds, whites only

4 ribs celery, cut into 1″ slices

4 Stuttgarter onions, if fresh, retain 2″ of stem and cut lengthwise; dried or cured, peel and cut in half

2 Tbsp. olive oil

½ c. apple cider

½ c. raw, unfiltered apple cider vinegar

½ c. red wine

2 qt. beef stock, or less

2 sprigs rosemary

Brine beef and refrigerate overnight; in the morning, strain and pat dry. Let beef rest ½ hour, season with salt and pepper.

Preheat oven to 400°.

Toss vegetables with olive oil; layer in roasting pan or Dutch oven. Cook until vegetables begin to brown; leave in pan and set aside. Lower oven to 225°.

In skillet, brown all sides of beef. Remove beef from skillet; deglaze pan with apple cider, vinegar, wine, and ½ cup of beef stock. Bring to a boil and reduce liquid by half; set aside.

Mix vegetables with sea salt and pepper; nestle beef into the center of the vegetables; place a sprig of rosemary at the front and back of the roast. Add beef broth to cover halfway up the side of beef. Cover and cook 3 hours, or until an internal temperature of 130° is reached.

Remove from oven. Keep covered and let sit for 20 minutes to continue cooking and letting the beef rest. Slice and serve with roasted pan vegetables. Ladle deglazed liquid over the sliced roast; reserve the remainder for a soup broth.

To serve cold (great for salads)—chill overnight and cut into ¼″ slices once fully chilled.

> **CHEF'S NOTE:** This recipe requires a hindquarter roast. We use one-third of the knuckle face, but any hindquarter oven roast can be used. Because of the lack of intramuscular fats in these primal cuts, we've been playing around with brining this cut much like we would briskets or hams. Other sweet onions can be substituted for the Stuttgarters.

CARROTS: A KITCHEN STAPLE

Plant them too close together and they are skinny and become forked. Too far apart, and the yield is not enough. They take a long time to germinate, and they need a lot of irrigation. They have to be regularly weeded or they fork. Their germination is slow.

And then there's the dirt.

"Carrots are funny; that dirt will stain them in no time," says Debbie Athearn, who wants every vegetable to be in its best form at the stand, not only in taste but also aesthetically. "You have to wash them as quickly as possible." They are the first thing to come off the truck after a harvest, and the first vegetable to get hosed down.

As commonplace as the vegetable seems to be, it is an essential building block for many dishes in the Morning Glory kitchen. Chef Robert and the kitchen crew use a whole lot of them. Along with celery, onions, and other vegetable variations like the leek, it is a component of mirepoix, the chopped-vegetable base for stocks, sauces, and braises. Carrots help lend body, complexity, and aroma to the other vegetable or protein characters that enter the dish. Carrots can be the main component of a dish, too, such as roasted carrots or carrot soup. They are juiced to add sweet flavor, creamy texture, and aroma to drinks at the juice bar, and are used in various ways at the salad bar.

Summer Brined Picnic Ham

BRINING

1 gal. Basic Meat Brine
(recipe, page 39)

2 c. peaches, chopped and pitted

½ c. brown sugar

1 inch fresh ginger, coarsely
chopped

1 picnic ham, 4 quartered, 5–6 lb.
bone and skin intact

HAM

2 onions, coarsely chopped

4 carrots, coarsely chopped

2 ribs celery, coarsely chopped

1 bulb fennel, cored, coarsely
chopped

¼ c. coarse mustard

4 sprigs sage

2 sprigs rosemary

1 c. apple cider, or any juice such
as orange

1 inch ginger, halved

2 peaches, pitted and chopped (or
skim the peach and ginger from
the brine)

2 qts. water or chicken broth

In large bowl or bucket, mix brine, peaches, sugar, and ginger. Add ham; cover and refrigerate overnight, 12 hours.

Preheat oven to 300°.

Remove ham from brine, pat dry, place in a high-sided roasting pan or Dutch oven.

Place onions, carrots, celery, fennel, mustard, sage, and rosemary around ham; add cider, ginger, peaches, and water or broth.

Cover and roast 3½–4 hours or until internal temperature reaches 180°. (The higher temperature allows for the breakdown of fat and connective tissue.)

Remove ham from pan and let cool. Peel back the skin. The ham can be separated at the muscles from the bone; slice. If you wish to serve warm, place slices back in the pan with the liquid and vegetables and heat 20–25 minutes.

> **CHEF'S NOTE:** This is a great dish for a beach or backyard meal: just slice, add a salad, maybe some corn bread (recipe, page 33) and you have a delicious meal.

MAKING HAY WHILE THE SUN SHINES

The sky is vast and cloudless, with a thin veil of haze over uninterrupted blue. Below, piles of hay form a pattern of concentric circles across thirty acres, a pale, dry field of yellow and brown. One tractor, two trucks, and nine farmers circle the field, baling hay and loading it into the truck beds.

"Don't ever hit the brake!" yells Ryan Cuene to the truck driver. Ryan, a second-year member of the field crew, stands high in the air, on top of stacks of hay bales in the back of the truck. A sudden brake could cause him to loose footing and fall.

This is the final process of haying. Three farmers walk beside the truck, picking up bales and tossing them to the stacker. Their vigilance is required, to snatch up any bale in the truck's path so it does not need to stop or drive over. As they are tossed, the stacker quickly puts them into place, building a platform sturdy enough to stay put across fourteen miles of Martha's Vineyard roads between Katama and Chilmark, where hay is stored. The stacker's job is to be a master builder and savvy architect.

Hay feeds Morning Glory's cattle most of the year. It supplements green-grasses during the warm months and is their sole sustenance when fresh grass is unavailable. The Athearns make hay from about forty acres of fields across the Island. Making good hay, and ensuring its nutritional quality—properly mowed, dried, and stored, as well as diversity of species—are essential elements of the herd's health.

Like other harvests, hay harvest is about finding that moment of readiness: high grasses with green seed heads and legumes in early bloom. The grasses should be mowed in the afternoon, because that is when they contain the most nutrients.

But hay is trickier than other harvests, because the grasses need to dry in the field before they can be baled. If not dry enough, hay will heat and mold in storage or start a fire from the heat produced as it ferments. If too dry, hay loses nutrients. Before mowing, the Athearns check the forecast. The hay needs three to four days of dry weather. When the moment is right, Dan, Simon, or Jim head out to mow.

It's a job that all the Athearn men enjoy.

"Mowing hay is probably the best job on the farm," says Simon. "It's beautiful, it smells great, and you're in a field, alone. It feels productive, like you're really getting a lot of value. You get to see tons of wildflowers, the butterflies are active, and the little baby deer are often parked nearby. It's very pleasing."

Over the next few days, the hay is worked in several ways with different tractor implements: it gets flipped from one side to the other, a process called tedding. Then it is raked into windrows, and finally formed into bales. By the time it is baled, it needs to get inside, quickly. Left overnight, another dew will dampen it, requiring labor to flip and dry it again

Even in ninety-degree weather, with a long afternoon of heavy work ahead, the field crew finds fun in the job. They crank up the music, and chill out with water from the yellow and red igloo cooler in their cargo.

Once the truck bed is stacked seven or eight bales high, Ryan hops off and heads toward the igloo. Someone else will stack the next truck, and he'll drive. "One thing I enjoy about farming is that I like to be able to see what I've created," says Ryan. "I just got done stacking that truck. That's always rewarding."

GREENS
A Bounty of Colors and Shapes

Edible greens are everywhere at Morning Glory. They are shiso and nasturtium in the herb garden. They are the waist high, frilly beds of curly leaf kale. They are the leaves that bundle tightly and form a head of cabbage: purple and green, conical caraflex or wrinkly savoy.

They grow on the tops of carrots and beets, radishes, and kohlrabi. They are even growing, unsolicited, between rows of cultivated plants: these are purslane and lamb's quarters, also known as weeds. The occasional customer will ask for these weeds, because they are not only high in nutrients but also have strong culinary appeal.

Whether they are wild weeds, cultivated plants, or the tops of root vegetables, all greens are leaves, one of the six major plant organs (along with root, stem, flower, seed, and fruit). Their structure, thin and flat, enables them to receive air and sunlight, and convert it into energy to keep the plant alive. Because the role of leaves is to use sunlight, powerful and potentially damaging to cells, to convert air and water into food, greens contain antioxidant compounds that protect them from harmful rays. These compounds contribute to the pigment and flavor of the green, making a leaf darker or richer green, purple or red, bitter or peppery.

Walk along the back shelf of the farm stand, and you will see greens in their many forms. You buy one over the other depending on your familiarity or your dinner plans. Cooked or raw? Steamed or sautéed? Accompaniment to eggs or meat? Maybe you plan to ferment some cabbage for sauerkraut.

As varied as greens look and taste, they are reminders that the members of a single family can look and behave very differently. It is clear from all the varieties of greens that a colorful "greens" salad is not an oxymoron.

The tops of vegetables are equally at home in some dishes. Beet greens and radish greens hold up well to heat: their flavors mellow, their textures soften. Try them raw, or add them to your smoothie. The radish greens will give it a kick, and the beet greens will impart their deep chlorophyll hue. Never heard of eating carrot tops? Chef Robert likes to add them to stocks.

Bulgur and Swiss Chard

SPECIAL EQUIPMENT: 6-QT. SAUCEPAN WITH LID, CAST-IRON SKILLET / SERVINGS: 4

2 c. water

1 tsp. sea salt, divided

1 c. bulgur, coarse #3

2 Tbsp. extra virgin olive oil

1 leek, white only, cut lengthwise, sliced at an angle, ¼″ strips

1 tsp. lemon thyme, or regular thyme, finely minced

¼ tsp. red chili flakes, and/or dash hot sauce

1 bunch Swiss chard, 8–10 leaves, stemmed and chopped across

⅛ tsp. lemon zest

1 Tbsp. fresh lemon juice

1 Tbsp. parsley, coarsely chopped

Bring water and ½ tsp. salt to a boil in 6-qt. saucepan, add bulgur, cover and reduce heat to simmer, cook 15 minutes.

Meanwhile, heat olive oil in seasoned cast-iron skillet over medium-high heat. Add leeks, remaining salt, thyme, chili flakes, if using, and chard stems; sauté 5 minutes, until leeks are soft, but not brown. Add chard leaves and stir continuously for 3 minutes, until wilted. Add lemon zest, lemon juice, and hot sauce, if using; cook 2–3 minutes until leaves are soft.

Fluff bulgur, fold into chard mixture, and add parsley. Serve warm.

CROP NOTES: Swiss chard: *Young stems are tender enough to be used along with the leaves. Mature plant stems are like a celery stalk; they should be trimmed like the leek, and sautéed with the leeks. Any number of leafy green varieties may be used in addition to or in place of the Swiss chard. Some such as mature collards or kale will require additional cooking time; others like mature arugula or mustard will wilt more readily. A quality apple cider vinegar or pickled rhubarb would be a nice "local" substitute for the lemon juice.*

Komatsuna Greens and Egg Sauté

SPECIAL EQUIPMENT: HEAVY-BOTTOM SAUTÉ PAN / SERVINGS: 2–3

6 farm eggs

½ c. whole milk

1 Tbsp. sour cream, optional

1 Tbsp. lard or extra virgin olive oil

2 small Stuttgarter onions, fresh or cured, finely sliced

1 bunch komatsuna greens

1 tsp. dill, finely minced

1 pinch nutmeg

¼ tsp. sea salt

1 pinch black pepper

1 dash hot sauce

Displayed side by side, bok choy, tatsoi, and komatsuna all have juicy, edible stems and crisp, quick-cooking leaves. Many people separate the leaf from stem, adding the stem to a sauté first, allotting it an extra few minutes to soften. Others brush the greens and stems with oil, sprinkle with sea salt, and grill them whole.

Preheat oven to 400°.

In bowl, beat eggs. Whisk in milk and sour cream, if using, until fully incorporated. Set aside.

In heavy-bottom sauté pan, melt lard or heat oil over medium heat, add onions, and cook 3–5 minutes.

Meanwhile, separate top third of greens, the leaf ends, and set aside. Slice stems in ⅓″ pieces; add to onions at the 3-minute point. Continue sautéing. While onions and stems are cooking, cut leaf ends into thin ribbons. Add to pan when onions begin to soften. Add dill, nutmeg, salt, pepper, and hot sauce. Mix to incorporate.

Pour egg mixture over greens, and cook over stove 2 minutes. Place in oven; bake 10 minutes, until top is firm and may just begin to brown.

CROP NOTES: *Topping the eggs with cheese prior to placing in the oven will add a richness to the dish. The tangy flavor and smooth melting quality of Spring Brook Farm "Reading", a Raclette style from Vermont, is a great addition.* **Leaf spinach:** *An appropriate substitution for the komatsuna, the stems of mature leaves may be too fibrous to include.* **Onions:** *Other sweet onions can be substituted for the Stuttgarters.*

Three Grains, Three Greens, One (Warm) Salad

SPECIAL EQUIPMENT: LARGE SKILLET / SERVINGS: 4

1 c. cooked golden quinoa

1 c. cooked brown rice

1 c. cooked whole-wheat couscous

2 Tbsp. extra virgin olive oil

1 medium leek, white only, cut ¼″ rings

1 medium yellow onion, julienned

½ tsp. fennel seed, or fresh anise hyssop

⅛ tsp. red chili flakes

3 sprigs fresh thyme, finely minced

½ tsp. sea salt

4 oz. shiitake mushrooms, stemmed, sliced if large

2 bunches greens: Swiss chard, curly leaf kale, Lacinato kale, collard greens, or beet greens; any combination, stemmed and ripped into 1½″–2″ pieces

4 Tbsp. warm water

2 Tbsp. miso

First, cook your grains.

Heat olive oil in skillet over medium heat.

Sauté leeks, onions, fennel seed, chili flakes, thyme, and diced stems, if using. Sprinkle with salt and stir occasionally, cooking until soft, about 10–12 minutes.

Add mushrooms, cook until soft, 4–5 minutes. Add greens, cook until fully wilted, 6–8 minutes. Remove from heat.

Meanwhile, in small bowl, mix warm water and miso. Hot water will kill live enzymes and cold water will not dissolve miso.

Mix together grains and greens. Let cool slightly. Add miso dressing, mix until evenly coated. Serve with Molasses Chicken (recipe, page 40).

> **CHEF'S NOTE:** On preparing greens: In this recipe, strip the kale and collards from the stem. For the chard and beet greens, cut off stem beyond leaf. The rest, what runs through the leaf can be used together with the leaf. Roll greens into a cocoon shape, horizontally; cut ½″ strips from top to bottom, then across through the center. Removed stems can be diced into ¼″ pieces, to be sautéed with the leeks and aromatics, adding nutrition and quantity to the dish and creating less waste.

CROP NOTES: *This dish uses three different whole grains. All these grains have different cooking times, so leftover cooked grains or a single grain would work well here. One of the keys to easily preparing delicious meals is to have some of the basics already prepared in the refrigerator. Whenever cooking a grain, make double the amount for extra on hand.*

Lentils and Kale

3 c. liquid, water or stock

1 c. dark green or French lentils

1 bay leaf

1 clove garlic

1¼ tsp. sea salt, divided

¼ tsp. black pepper

2 Tbsp. extra virgin olive oil

⅛ tsp. red chili flakes

½ tsp. ground cumin

1 tsp. fresh thyme, minced

2 medium carrots, medium dice

1 rib celery, medium dice

1 small onion, medium dice

½ bulb fennel, cored, medium dice

1 bunch kale, 8–10 leaves, ribs removed, leaf coarsely chopped in ½″ pieces

¼ c. raw, unfiltered apple cider vinegar or water

1 Tbsp. coarse Dijon mustard

1 Tbsp. fresh herbs

Bring liquid, lentils, bay leaf, ¼ tsp. salt, pepper, and garlic to a boil in 6-qt. saucepan. Reduce heat and simmer 20–25 minutes. Lentils should be neither crunchy nor soft.

Meanwhile, preheat skillet over medium heat. Add oil, chili flakes, cumin, and thyme. Stir to season the oil. Add carrots, celery, onion, and fennel; cook until vegetables soften, 15 minutes.

Add kale, stirring to fully incorporate the kale. As kale begins to wilt, add the remaining ¼ cup vinegar or water so kale does not stick to the skillet. Stir constantly.

Strain lentils and poor over kale; stir in mustard. Let sit 2 minutes, then season with salt and pepper. At this point, 1 Tbsp. any fresh herbs, such as dill or parsley, can be folded in. Serve warm.

CHEF'S NOTE: We prefer the dark green or French variety of lentil in this recipe, as it maintains its structural integrity. A great item for soups and salads.

CROP NOTES: *Early season or young kale will cook much more quickly and soften much more than mature leaves; the mature leaves will often retain the frilly edges incorporating the lentils. Softer, leafy green vegetables will seemingly disappear here, though their flavor will be fine.*

Turnip, Broccoli, and Kohlrabi Greens

1 lb. trimmed leaves, turnip, broccoli, and kohlrabi

2 Tbsp. extra virgin olive oil

1 leek, medium dice

1 onion, medium dice

1 pinch anise seed

1 pinch celery seed

1 pinch red chili flakes

1 tsp. lemon juice

Sea salt

Pepper

To prepare leaves, fold in half to expose spine; remove spine lengthwise throughout the leaves and discard. Stack leaves on top of each other and cut across into thin ribbons.

Over medium-high heat, heat oil in heavy-bottom skillet. Add leek, onion, and seasonings. Add greens, stirring to coat with hot oil; cook 3–8 minutes until leaves begin to soften. Season with salt, pepper, and lemon juice. Toss and cook 1 minute.

Alternatively, when leaves are more mature, substitute half the oil with bacon fat or lard. The leaves will require a longer cooking time, 8–12 minutes. Add 1 pinch each of mustard and caraway seeds.

CROP NOTES: *The large, coarse greens of our vegetables are often discarded, but they are at least as delectable as their "showier" counterparts. Early in the season, we treat the greens as we would Swiss chard by separating leaf from stem at the base of the leaf. As the plants develop and mature the leaves toughen and we treat them more like collard greens, removing and discarding the stalk and spine. The hardier greens require a longer cooking time and more moisture in the form of fat or oil.*

LACTO WHAT?

Lacto-fermentation is really canning for beginners. It is the process that produces traditional dill pickles, kimchi, and real sauerkraut. It takes nothing more than salt, vegetables, and water—no canning, no fancy equipment.

It's also been around for centuries. Pioneer households often had crocks of sauerkraut, lacto-fermented cucumber pickles, and other treasures such as beets, onions, or garlic waiting out the winter in the root cellar. And people in other countries have often used this simple method of preserving food; kimchi from Korea and cortido from Latin America are just two.

Lacto-Fermented Cabbage

SPECIAL EQUIPMENT: NONREACTIVE OPEN-TOPPED CONTAINER OR CROCK, FOOD PROCESSOR, CANNING JARS / YIELD: FIVE 6-QT. CONTAINERS

Cabbage, 2 large or 3 medium heads

2 sea salt, or more

Well or true spring water

SEASONINGS

1 Tbsp. fennel, caraway, celery, coriander, anise, and/or mustard seeds

½ c. white vinegar

2 small dried chilies, soaked in boiling vinegar prior to adding

2 tsp. freshly grated horseradish, soaked in boiling vinegar prior to adding

ADDITIONS
Reduce amount of cabbage to equal amount of other vegetables added

Beets

Carrots

Daikon

Scarlet or Hakuri turnips

Other cabbage varieties

Quarter and core cabbage. Using food processor fitted with slicing attachment, shred cabbage.

In large mixing bowl, add 3 c. cabbage; sprinkle with 1 tsp. salt. Repeat until all cabbage has been salted in the bowl. Add all seasonings to the cabbage and vigorously massage cabbage up to 10 minutes. Water should begin to accumulate in the bottom of bowl.

Place cabbage in sterilized crock; press down firmly to remove all trapped air. Continue to apply pressure until cabbage is covered by ½″ of the accumulated water. If dry, let cabbage rest for 30 minutes. Apply pressure again. If still not covered, slowly add spring water to cover cabbage by ½″.

Place sterilized weight on top of cabbage, ensuring the liquid barrier remains. Cover and refrigerate 2–3 weeks. An airtight seal is not necessary.

Spoon off any scum on the surface and place in sterilized jars; each jar should have sufficient water to cover cabbage. Close jars and refrigerate. Do not use hot water process jars. Refrigeration will suffice and ensure the cultures remain vibrant.

Warm Caraflex Cabbage and Apples

SPECIAL EQUIPMENT: HEAVY-BOTTOM SAUCEPAN WITH LID / SERVINGS: 4 SIDE-DISH SIZES

2 Tbsp. extra virgin olive oil

¼ tsp. caraway seed

½ tsp. mustard seed

¼ tsp. fennel seeds

¼ tsp. red chili flakes

1 medium onion, halved, finely julienned

1 leek, white only, halved, finely julienned

½ tsp. sea salt

¼ tsp. black pepper

½ tsp. thyme, finely minced

1 tsp. fresh sage

1 Caraflex cabbage, quartered, cored, sliced across or shredded in food processor

2 golden delicious apples, cored, peeled, slice in half moons

¼ c. raw, unfiltered apple cider vinegar

1 Tbsp. herbed mustard

½ c. apple cider

Heat oil over medium heat in sauce pan. Add caraway, mustard and fennel seeds and chili flakes. Add onion, leeks, salt, and pepper and cook 8–10 minutes until soft. Add herbs and cook 1 minute, stir in cabbage and apples to coat with oil mixture. Add vinegar, mustard and cider. Cover pan, cook 3–5 minutes, allowing the cabbage to steam and begin to soften.

CHEF'S NOTE: Serve this with Brined Beef Brisket (recipe, page 49) for a great meal.

CROP NOTES: Caraflex Cabbage: *With its odd conical shape, this item has become a favorite in the kitchen. It has a subtle sweetness with little grassy overtones. The tender leaves lend themselves to raw, as well as lightly cooked, cabbage recipes, such as here. The leaves are strong enough, however, to hold up to being stuffed, rolled, and baked. When just harvested, the head is dense with residual moisture and will require little additional moisture during cooking.* **Apples:** *The aroma of the Island golden delicious apples tops the charts among any variety we carry. While the apple retains a nice texture, it is because of the lasting aroma that it finds itself here. Instead of substituting with a red delicious, choose a honey crisp or pink lady instead.*

Brown Rice, Bok Choy, and Chickpea Miso

SPECIAL EQUIPMENT: 6-QT. SAUCEPAN WITH LID / SERVINGS: 2

2 ¼ c. water

½ tsp. sea salt, plus a pinch

1 c. short-grain brown rice

1 bunch of mature bok choy

1 Tbsp. chickpea miso, mixed with
   2 Tbsp. warm water

2 tsp. toasted sesame seeds

1 Tbsp. minced cilantro

Dash of Morning Glory's Mellow
   Yellow chili sauce

Bring water to boil in 6-qt. saucepan. Add a pinch of sea salt. Add rice, cover, and reduce to a simmer for 40 minutes.

Meanwhile, separate leaves from stems of bok choy. Place leaves on top of each other and cut across in ¼ to ½˝ slices. Continue slicing same width across the stems.

Five minutes prior to rice being finished, uncover and pack in choy on top of the rice. Cover for an additional 3 to 5 minutes to allow the end cooking time to steam the choy above the rice. Check at 3 minutes. Choy is done when it is completely softened and stems have begun to offer just a bit of give.

Add 1 Tbsp. of miso mixed with 2 Tbsp. of warm water. Add sesame seeds and cilantro. Stir thoroughly. Fold in a dash of hot sauce.

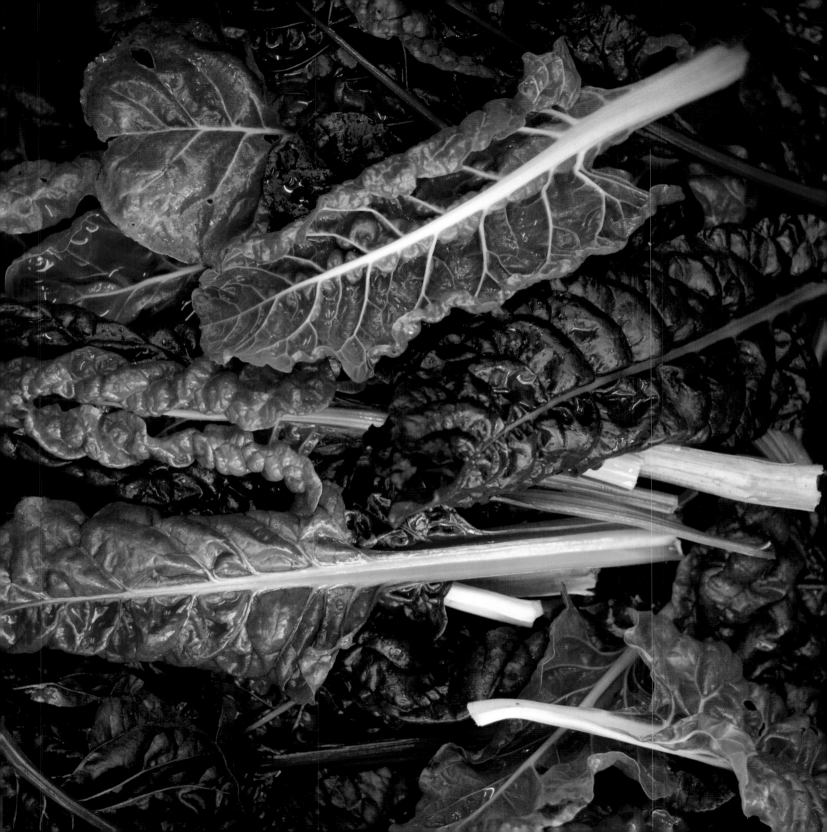

Rainbow Chard, Bacon, and Cheese Quiche

1 prepared pie crust (recipe, page 184)

8 oz. bacon, cut into small chunks

1 small yellow onion, diced

6 c. chopped rainbow chard (about ½ bunch)

5 oz. brie, cut into small chunks

8 eggs

⅓ c. milk or fat-free half-and-half

2 tsp. chopped fresh thyme

½ tsp. salt

¼ tsp. ground black pepper

Recipe contributed by Barbara Leckerling of Chappaquiddick.

Heat oven to 450°.

Unroll the pie crust and set into a pie pan, crimping and trimming as needed to form an even edge. Set aside.

In a large skillet over medium-high heat, combine the bacon, onion, and chard. Cook until the chard has wilted and released water, about 6 minutes.

Let the bacon mixture cool slightly, then use a slotted spoon to transfer it to the crust, arranging it in an even layer. Scatter the brie evenly over it.

In a large bowl, whisk together the eggs, milk, thyme, salt, and pepper.

Pour the egg mixture into the pie crust, then bake for 25 minutes, or until puffed and set at the center and lightly browned at the edges. If the crust browns too quickly, use strips of foil to cover the edges.

> **CHEF'S NOTE:** This recipe calls for brie cheese, but I recommend substituting Springbrook Reading, a wonderful melting cheese from Vermont that is carried both at Morning Glory and in other fine cheese stores.

Bay Scallops and Braised Greens

SPECIAL EQUIPMENT: WELL-SEASONED CAST-IRON PAN / SERVINGS: 2

1 Tbsp. extra virgin olive oil

1 leek, white only, ¼" dice or ½ c. leeks ragout (recipe, page 14)

½ tsp. tarragon, freshly chopped

1 Tbsp. canola oil, or other high-heat oil

1 lb. bay scallops

¼ tsp. sea salt

1 pinch ground black pepper

1 bunch mizuna greens

1 bunch red frills mustard greens, washed thoroughly and cut and torn into 3" pieces

1 bunch arugula

Pinch coarse sea salt

Bring pan up to temperature at medium heat. Add the olive oil.

Sauté leeks (or use leeks ragout), stirring often until soft. Sprinkle in tarragon and scrape the pan's contents into a bowl.

Return heat to medium high and add the canola oil.

Season the scallops with salt and pepper. Wait for 20–30 seconds or until the pan is uniformly hot.

Carefully add the scallops to the pan. Let them sear without stirring until they begin to caramelize and turn a deep golden brown on the seared side. Toss the pan to loosen the scallops.

Add the leek mixture, toss, and spoon into a serving dish.

Place the greens in the hot pan, toss quickly to just wilt the leaves, and place over the scallops.

Sprinkle with coarse sea salt.

CHEF'S NOTE: Choose a strong, peppery olive oil for this recipe.

Basic Pickling Brine

2 ½ c. raw, unfiltered apple cider
   vinegar or white vinegar

1 Tbsp. fine sea salt

½ c. organic evaporated cane juice
   or natural sugar crystals

¼ tsp. celery seed

½ tsp. mustard seed

¼ tsp. red chili flakes

Combine all ingredients in a 6-qt. stainless-steel pot.

At medium-high heat, whisk ingredients together until sugar and salt are fully dissolved.

Yield 3 cups, and will cover 3 quarts solid vegetable to make 6 pint-size containers.

LETTUCE
The Enduring and Endearing Crop

Lettuce is one of the first and last crops grown and sold at the farm stand. Some locals even buy it before the stand reopens in the spring, directly from the greenhouses.

The lettuce display in the stand is intriguing, like a work of art with all its shades of red and green and its textural diversity. Not only is it attractive, but lettuce is also eternally popular. On a slow day, one hundred heads will come out of the fields; on a busy one, the lettuce crew will pick a thousand.

And it has held endless fascination for at least one crew member at Morning Glory Farm, who has returned year after year precisely to work with lettuce.

As a fifteen-year-old boy, Andrew Valenti got a job at Morning Glory Farm, picking up cut heads of lettuce and putting them in a box. Nine years later and with a tattoo of Nancy Butterhead lettuce on his shoulder, he is still harvesting and washing lettuce.

Every morning, Andrew starts his day with lettuce harvest. He often works with another person, who becomes his second in command. Together they walk the rows and cut the stems with small knives. Afterward, they retrace their steps with baskets, and squeeze heads the size of a lion's mane together with seventeen others. They squeak and contract against the other heads, shrinking to the size of a slender romaine.

Inevitably, some of the lettuce in the field has bolted. When a head begins to flower, it turns bitter and grows vertically, like a Christmas tree. The red Dodge Dakota Sport that is the lettuce truck is perpetually festive, with a bolted red head sticking up from either side of the truck bed. Andrew calls this the Lettuce Parade.

Andrew's respect for the vegetable is apparent in the way he has transformed the washing process. During his first year working with lettuce, under the instruction of a man he calls his lettuce guru, full trays of lettuce were dumped into a sink of water. The water quickly became filthy and the sinks needed frequent refilling. Now, he removes dead leaves from each head and cuts off excess stem. He dunks them, one by one, into a full sink, then tips the head upside down to drain it. The dirt sinks to the bottom, and the heads go out to the stand healthy and cleaned of extra dirt. Washing the leaves at home once they are separated is still necessary.

Morning Glory grows four types of lettuce, and several varieties of each. *Loose-leaf* types seem to have flow, with many tender, curvy leaves loosely attached to a central stem. *Bibb* lettuce has a characteristically tight, bundled heart that looks like a small cabbage. Crisp, light green Butterhead seems to be the most well-known name within the Bibb type. Juicy, crunchy Iceberg lettuce is a *crisphead* variety, and Romaine is a lettuce type itself, also knows as *cos.* Newer to the Morning Glory repertoire are eight different kinds of salanova, nonheading lettuces that are cored, cleaned, and sold as the baby lettuce mix.

ARUGULA

Although technically a green, arugula is known in some places as salad rocket—a fitting description of the peppery plant that can add zest to any dish where it is used. Arugula, small in size but powerfully peppery, is sold loose, in a wooden barrel. It can be a salad, enhance a salad, or wilt with a quick hit of heat and oil.

Throw it into a green smoothie for an extra kick of flavor, and add it to sandwiches just as you would lettuce.

Arugula or Sweet Pea Pesto

½ lb. loose arugula leaves (thoroughly washed)

⅔ c. garlic oil or extra virgin olive oil

1 Tbsp. roasted garlic, or 3 cloves

¼ c. parmesan cheese, grated (sub a hard sheep's milk cheese for extra zing)

1 Tbsp. lemon juice

½ tsp. lemon zest

¼ tsp. sea salt

Combine all ingredients in food processor and process until smooth.

We recommend placing in two 8-oz. containers. This will keep in the refrigerator for three weeks or in the freezer for an extended period of time. To defrost, simply place container, still covered, in refrigerator for two days.

> **CHEF'S NOTE:** Although ratios will alter sometimes given differences in water content, this recipe is open to a seemingly numerous variety of options. While whole peas benefit from a 30- to 45-second blanching in boiling water, other substitutions, such as arugula, are best raw. This is a great location for arugula as it begins to mature.

VARIATION: *Sweet Pea Pesto*

¼ lb. shelled peas or whole English peas, blanched, chilled, and dry; or ¼ lb. arugula leaves

2 Tbsp. extra virgin olive oil

2 Tbsp. sheep or goat's milk hard cheese, grated. Accessible variety is pecorino romano, but there are spectacular New England varieties available

1 Tbsp. Roasted Garlic, 3 cloves (recipe, page 51)

¼ tsp. lemon zest

Place all ingredients in food processor, process until smooth. If still clumpy, add additional olive oil. Set aside.

CROP NOTES: Arugula: *This recipe is a great outlet for mature, peppery leaves and stems.* **Other greens/herbs:** *The basic ratio of this recipe will work for any number of different crops from basil, cilantro, bell peppers, cooked beets. . . . Some of our favorites include cilantro with almonds and tangy sheep's milk cheese, bell peppers (even better roasted) with oregano, and dill with roasted sweet onions.*

Early Summer Salad

1 c. Roasted Pumpkin Seeds (recipe, page 128) or sunflower seeds

2 oz. pea sprouts, 2–4″

8 oz. mixed baby greens

½ c. English peas, stems removed; slice ¼″ angled pieces

2 apricots, halved, pitted, cut in 8–12 slices

2 oz. shaved New England hard sheep's or goat's milk cheese

1 c. Russian Beet Salad (recipe, page 143)

Prepare pumpkin seeds ahead of time.

Salad can be composed by placing greens on the plate first, then layering the ingredients. Or toss ingredients to combine.

Suggested dressing: Stuttgarter Onion Vinaigrette (recipe, page 85).

THE LETTUCE TRAIN

Like many farm crops, lettuce starts its life in the greenhouse before being transplanted into the fields. Lettuce transplanting is a fun sight to watch. The field crew makes a human transplanting machine. Their movements are practiced and swift.

The "droppers" walk backward, slowly, with trays of lettuce seedlings in hand. The three planters follow, crawling shoulder to shoulder along the plant bed in a synchronized fashion, devouring the seedlings that the droppers leave for them: indent, plant, pinch, indent, plant, pinch.

Their hands move so fast that their motions become a blur. They move along until they reach the end of a row, and left in their trace are frilly little leaves, orderly and bright.

Here green, there red, the rows look like a candy necklace with its intervals of color.

Arugula or Sweet Pea Pesto Panini

SPECIAL EQUIPMENT: PANINI PRESS OR NONSTICK PAN / SERVINGS: 2

**Arugula or Sweet Pea Pesto
(recipe, page 77)**

2 oz. cheddar cheese, sliced

1 tomato, thinly sliced

4 slices 100% whole-wheat bread

Recipe contributed by Vineyard Nutrition

Warm panini grill or nonstick pan on medium heat.

Layer pesto, cheese, tomato, and more cheese between two slices of bread.

Spray panini grill or pan with cooking spray. Place sandwich on grill/pan; cook until cheese melts, turn once if using pan.

Noman's Island Dressing

½ c. cottage cheese

½ c. sour cream

¼ c. mayonnaise

8 oz. ketchup

2 Tbsp. parsley, finely chopped

1 Tbsp. dill, finely chopped

1 Tbsp. chives, finely chopped

½ tsp. sea salt

¼ tsp. black pepper

¼ tsp. lemon zest

5 oz. or ½ jar of Morning Glory Farm bread and butter pickles, equal parts brine and pickle

Combine all ingredients, except pickles, in food processor, including brine from pickles. Process until smooth and fully incorporated. Add pickles, and pulse until pickles are broken down, but remain chunky.

Keep in a sealed container in refrigerator up to 3 weeks.

CHEF'S NOTE: This style dressing is great for curly kale leaves, crisp head lettuce, or fresh cabbage. Avoid using it for fragile baby leaf mixes, baby arugula, or other delicate leaves. Although the three herbs selected here are available for most of the season, many different combinations would work fine: oregano, sage, cilantro, chervil, tarragon. We keep this dressing in production throughout the year.

Farm Herb Vinaigrette

⅛ c. sage, coarsely chopped, ½ bunch from Morning Glory Farm

⅛ c. English thyme, ½ bunch from Morning Glory Farm

¼ c. parsley, coarsely chopped, ¼ bunch from Morning Glory Farm

¼ tsp. lemon zest

½ tsp. sea salt

¼ tsp. black pepper

¼ c. white or raw, unfiltered apple cider vinegar

1 Tbsp. smooth Dijon mustard

1 ½ c. extra virgin olive oil

In blender or food processor, add herbs, lemon zest, salt, pepper, vinegar, and Dijon mustard. Pulse to shred herbs; scrape down sides. Add oil; blend until completely combined.

Will store in sealed container in refrigerator up to 3 weeks.

CROP NOTES: *The notation under ingredients for herb quantities acknowledges that our herb bunches are not consistent with standard retail sizes. Any number of home substitutes would be appropriate.*

Stuttgarter Onion Vinaigrette

1 lb. Stuttgarter onions, 5 small to medium, aged, substitute white or yellow

1 ¼ c. + 2 Tbsp. extra virgin olive oil, divided

¾ tsp. sea salt, divided

½ tsp. lavender, finely minced

½ tsp. summer savory or fresh rosemary

2 oz. sherry vinegar

2 oz. raw, unfiltered apple cider vinegar

¼ tsp. black pepper

Preheat oven to 425°.

Peel and halve onions, place cut side down on lined baking sheet. Drizzle with 2 Tbsp. olive oil. Sprinkle with ¼ tsp. salt. Roast until tops are golden brown and the insides are soft; the onion will give way to touch. Remove from oven and let cool.

In blender or food processor, mix lavender, savory, vinegars, salt, and pepper; blend until combined. Add onions and continue to blend. Drizzle in olive oil until the dressing is smooth and completely emulsified.

Will keep in sealed container in refrigerator up to 3 weeks, or properly jarred up to 1 year.

CHEF'S NOTE: For a lighter flavor and texture, use white vinegar and substitute a more neutral salad oil, like canola, for half of the olive oil.

CROP NOTES: Onion: *The higher moisture content of the fresh onions will lead to uneven roasting: we suggest the cured or dried instead. Substitute any sweet onion if Stuttgarter's aren't available.* **Lavender:** *A bold and unique flavor. We enjoy its combination with the roasted onion. If the flavor is too pronounced, sage or thyme would work well here.*

ONIONS: THE MOST COMPLEX OF PLANTS

Walk into the farm stand in June, shortly after it opens, and you will find
scallions, white tipped as well as magnificent fuchsia. Shortly behind scallions,
green onions make an appearance in the farm stand. In the South, a scallion is
a green onion. Morning Glory's green onions are quite a different crop.

Green onions are the chubby walla walla onions, along with other varieties. They don't
have a dry layer on the outside, as you'll see later on other onions. They are still immature,
still growing, and as a result they taste extra juicy and sweet—as sweet as a raw onion
can get. They should be kept in the fridge and eaten soon after they are picked.

As the summer days grow hotter and longer, the onion leaves, long and thin, start to yellow, then
brown. When the leaves are no longer green, the plants' bulbs are simply labeled "onions." Or
storage onions. Once the leaves have dried up, they wilt and come to rest on the ground. At that
point, the crew knows it's time for the big harvest. The onion is no longer growing, and, unlike
earlier harvests, every onion left in the ground gets picked. After that, they will be cured, or dried.

Arugula and Farro Warm Salad

SPECIAL EQUIPMENT: 6-QT. SAUCEPAN WITH LID, LARGE SKILLET / SERVINGS: 2–3

1 c. pearled farro

2 ¼ c. cold water

½ tsp. sea salt, plus pinch for water

2 Tbsp. olive oil or coconut oil

2 spring onions, chopped. Tops removed, 4″ stem reserved

1 leek, white only, chopped. Slice in half lengthwise, then across at ¼ inch

2 Tbsp. flat leaf parsley, coarsely chopped

1 Tbsp. oregano, finely chopped

⅛ tsp. black pepper

8 oz. mushrooms, sliced, any variety

⅛ tsp. ground nutmeg

1 Tbsp. raw, unfiltered apple cider vinegar

8 oz. arugula, stems removed

In a 6-qt. pot, place farro and 2 ¼ cup cold water and a pinch of salt. Bring to a boil, and reduce to simmer for 15–18 minutes.

In a heavy bottom skillet, heat the oil on medium-high heat, add onion, leek, parsley, and oregano. Season with salt and pepper, sauté for 5–8 minutes until the vegetables are soft but not browned.

Add mushrooms and nutmeg, cook an additional 5 minutes or until mushrooms soften and begin to brown.

Add the vinegar and the arugula. Toss vigorously to coat the arugula, 30 to 45 seconds. Remove from heat.

In a large bowl, add farro, mushroom and arugula mixture, and parsley. Mix all to incorporate.

Serve warm or chill for a great summer salad.

CHEF'S NOTE: Pearled farro will cook faster but will release more gluten—becoming sticky. Whole farro requires twice the cooking time, but kernels will not be sticky. Instead they will have a more pronounced grain or nutty flavor.

CROP NOTES: Arugula: *Use the more mature leaves for cooking applications such as this recipe and leave the younger, more tender leaves raw for salads.* **Spring onions:** *Any fresh, uncured onion may be substituted; the lighter, sweeter quality of a fresh onion works best in a dish such as this. Out of season, try scallions.* **Leeks:** *Available to us on the farm throughout our operation, wintered leeks harvested in the spring are simply beautiful, sweet, and full of flavor.* **Herbs:** *Many robust herbs such as savory, thyme, rosemary, or sage may be used instead of oregano. Likewise, lighter herbs like dill or cilantro may replace the parsley.*

PEACHES
Years and Years of Work

Six rows of peach trees live a couple minutes walk from the farm stand, and an even shorter distance from Jim and Debbie Athearn's house. Each row of trees produces a different variety of peach, some yellow fleshed, some white, all with a deep pink blush where the sun's rays contact the fruit.

Starting in mid-August several trees at a time drip with juicy, ripe fruit. The season continues until all forty-five peach trees have had their chance to produce seed, and the succulent fruit that surrounds it.

Jim Athearn planted the peach trees in 1992 on a half acre of land that had seen several transformations before becoming an orchard. He was interested in growing whatever could grow on the Island, in Edgartown, a microclimate of its own. He knew peaches could succeed, and when they did, they would be delicious, picked ripe, and "far better [tasting] than anything that gets shipped in," says Jim.

The Athearns expected to wait five years before getting a good crop of peaches, but it actually took eight years. Jim and Debbie consulted a University of Massachusetts graduate student to help them figure out why the peaches were failing to produce a crop. They were told they'd have to apply a fungicide to give the peaches a fighting chance against brown rot, which can infect the tree even before the fruit sets. It is the most common threat to stone fruit in New England, especially harmful in areas that are wet and humid, and can make a shriveled, brown mummy of a perfectly good peach. Jim didn't expect to need a fungicide to grow peaches, but the trees weren't fruiting, so he did his research and tested the advice.

Right away, they got a crop of peaches.

In recent years, Dan Athearn, Jim and Debbie's son, has been the primary caretaker of the orchard. Dan is the Peach Guy.

Standing in a peach tree six feet above the ground, Dan looks as comfortable out on a limb as he does on flat ground. With a harvest bucket strapped around his shoulders and hanging by his waist, his hands are free to assess the peaches for ripeness.

"It is kind of an emotional experience to pick a peach like that," says Dan, looking at an unblemished, yellow and pink fruit with a diameter as big as his palm. It is so ripe it releases itself from the stem with the slightest pull of Dan's hand. He adds it to the crate of salable peaches.

Roasted Chicken
with Roasted Peaches, Tomatoes, and Leeks

2 Tbsp. olive oil

1 tsp. butter

2 stalks celery, sliced

2 whole medium carrots, tops removed, cleaned, and sliced

1 medium onion, coarsely chopped

2 large leeks, white part only, sliced into rounds

1 tsp. fresh thyme, minced

sea salt

pepper

4 tomatoes, coarsely chopped

2 peaches, sliced

4 split breasts on the bone, skin on, or one whole chicken, halved or cut into parts

smoked paprika

GLAZE

½ c. orange juice, or juice of 2 oranges

2 Tbsp. honey

2 Tbsp. Dijon mustard

Dash of hot sauce or Morning Glory's Mellow Yellow chili sauce

Preheat the oven to 375°

Heat olive oil and butter over medium heat in a skillet. Add the celery, carrots, onions, leeks, and minced thyme. Sprinkle with two pinches of sea salt and four grinds of black pepper.

Sauté for 5 minutes.

Stir in tomatoes and peaches and immediately shut off heat.

Situate the chicken on top of the sautéed vegetables in a single layer.

Whisk together all the glaze ingredients in a bowl.

Brush on chicken or spoon over the top of the chicken. (Use only what you need; you won't need all the glaze.)

Sprinkle the chicken with a liberal sprinkle of salt, a grind of pepper, and a pinch of smoked paprika per chicken piece.

Cook for 45–50 minutes, basting every 15 minutes with the pan juices.

Gluten-Free Peach Cobbler

FRUIT FILLING

6 c. peach slices, 12 medium ripe peaches (you can peel or not, your choice)

½ c. maple syrup

1 Tbsp. tapioca starch

BISCUIT TOPPING

1 c. brown rice flour

1 c. white rice flour

⅔ c. potato starch

⅓ c. tapioca starch

4 tsp. xanthan gum

2 Tbsp. baking powder

1 tsp. baking soda

½ tsp. salt

2 Tbsp. sugar

1 c. shortening

1½ c. buttermilk

In a mixing bowl, toss the fruit with the maple syrup and tapioca starch. Transfer to a casserole dish, any shape. The fruit should be about an inch deep.

Preheat oven to 350°.

In a clean mixing bowl, combine all the dry ingredients, tossing to mix thoroughly. Cut in the shortening using a pastry cutter, forks, or your hands, until incorporated (mixture should be crumbly).

Pour in the buttermilk and mix until batter comes together; it will be damp and sticky. Spoon onto the prepared fruit.

Bake for 45 minutes, until topping is puffy and browned, and fruit is soft. (Use a thin knife or a skewer to test.)

Cool and serve.

> **CHEF'S NOTE:** This is a classic New England cobbler with a tender biscuit topping. This recipe works great with any soft ripe fruit in season—blueberry, strawberry, rhubarb, cranberry, Macintosh apple, etc. You might also try combinations— peach and blueberry is one of my favorites in the summer, and I love Macintosh and cranberry in the fall/winter.

Summer Peach Mojito

SPECIAL EQUIPMENT: TALL GLASS, MUDDLER / SERVINGS: 1

Small bunch mint (about 2 springs, including small, tender stems)

1 ripe peach, pitted and quartered

1 Tbsp. light brown sugar

½ oz. fresh lemon juice

½ oz. fresh lime juice

1 ½ oz. rum (Massachusetts' Bully Boy rum is fantastic and available locally)

¾ oz. St. Germaine liqueur

ice

club soda

Recipe contributed by cookbook author and home chef Catherine Walthers of Chilmark: "Summer fruit and herbs from the farm can be put to other good uses. I suggest experimenting with different herb combinations with the peaches as well, such as mint and basil, or basil and cilantro. All you need is a muddler, and great friends and farm food to enjoy this with."

In a tall Collins or iced tea glass, add mint, peach pieces, and brown sugar. With a muddler, gently mash the ingredients until pulpy.

Add the citrus juices, rum, and St. Germaine and stir. Fill glass with ice, top with club soda, and stir again to infuse the drink with the peach flavor.

Garnish with a mint sprig and lime wheel.

THE EASY WAY TO PEEL PEACHES

Bring a pot of water to a rolling boil. Meanwhile, prepare an ice-water bath.

Using a sharp paring knife, score an "x" into the bottom of each peach. Working in small batches, drop peaches into boiling water. Let boil 40 seconds; if peaches are on the hard side, boil up to 1 minute. Using slotted spoon, remove peaches and place into ice-water bath

Using clean fingers or paring knife, pull skin off starting at the scored "x."

Peach Jam

SPECIAL EQUIPMENT: CANDY THERMOMETER, LARGE HEAVY-BOTTOMED POT, CANNING JARS / YIELD: TWELVE 8 OZ. JARS

Always check safe canning methods at the National Center for Home Food Preservation, www.nchfp.uga.edu

2 Tbsp. powdered apple or crabapple pectin

¼ c. warm water

5 lb. fresh peaches, peeled

8 c. sugar

1 Tbsp. lemon juice

1 Tbsp. fresh ginger, grated (optional)

Dissolve pectin in warm water. Set aside.

Over medium-low heat, cook pealed peaches in heavy-bottomed pot until fruit is tender, 18–22 minutes.

Add sugar and lemon juice. Increase to medium-high heat; bring to a boil, stirring often. When mixture reaches 220°, whisk in pectin slurry and ginger, if using. Return to 220°, boil 2 minutes.

Remove from heat. Jam is ready to be canned in clean, sterilized jars.

CHEF'S NOTE: Serve with Downeast Biscuits for a special breakfast or dinner treat. (See recipe, page 96)

Downeast Biscuits

6 c. all-purpose flour, plus additional for rolling out

2 Tbsp. cream of tartar

1 Tbsp. baking soda

2 tsp. salt

8 oz. (2 sticks) unsalted butter, cold, cut into ½ to 1″ chunks

2¼ c. cold milk

Preheat oven to 425°.

In a medium mixing bowl, whisk together flour, cream of tartar, baking soda, and salt.

Toss cold butter in flour mixture, then cut butter into mixture using pastry cutter, forks, or fingers, looking for a shaggy consistency with flat lumps of butter.

Stir in cold milk just until combined—dough will look craggy and uneven.

Turn dough out onto a lightly floured surface, including any unincorporated dry ingredients that may still be in bowl.

Pat dough into a flat rectangle, then divide in half and layer one half over the other. Repeat once again: pat to flatten, divide, and layer. Roll or pat to desired thickness, about ¾″ to 1″ thick. Cut into desired shape.

Bake on parchment-lined baking sheet 14–16 minutes, turning pan halfway through for an even bake. Bake until tops are golden brown.

Remove from oven and brush with melted butter. Serve with honey or your favorite jam. (We like our peach jam, recipe, page 95.)

Variation: For a more savory biscuit, follow the recipe above but add 3 oz. sharp cheddar cheese, grated, and 2 Tbsp. chives, finely chopped, when you place all ingredients but butter into the bowl. Continue as above. Brush on buttermilk after cooking, and sprinkle the biscuit tops with 1 oz. more of grated cheese.

PEAS & BEANS
No Combine? No Problem

If there is ever a moment when the entrepreneurial spirit of the Athearn family shows itself clearly, it is happening now, in one of the farm's storage rooms.

Simon Athearn, pillowcases tied around his shoes, is stomping on the dried bean pods to separate beans from their pods. He has already passed the beans through a modified wood chipper, set to knock the pods around and break them up, without hurting the beans themselves. Once he finishes his pillow case dance, he will roll the beans and chaff down a piece of plywood set at an angle, so that the round, heavy beans will slide down while the lightweight chaff from the plant will remain on the plywood.

After that, Simon will drop the beans in front of a box fan, where any remaining chaff and debris will be blown away. What he will have left is seventy-five pounds of dried, storable beans.

This multistep process is far from the norm.

A machine exists for this kind of work and takes care of harvest, threshing, and winnowing. It's called a combine, and it's what large farms use for grain and beans alike. How else could dried and canned beans be so cheap? How else could animals be economically fattened on grain? Definitely not with a hand-cleaning process.

"It's one approach. It's not mechanized," Simon admits. "But as far as I can tell there's not much of middle ground between a two-hundred-thousand-dollar combine and me stomping on them on a clean, concrete floor."

But Morning Glory's dry bean process has come a long way in efficiency over the four years they have grown them. While it's still evolving, Simon would feel comfortable using the exact same method next year, even with double or triple the weight of beans. From pod to clean bean, the process took Simon one hour and ten minutes.

"I was timing myself to see if the crop's profitable," says Simon. "It's reasonably close." Until a combine arrives, the field crew will continue to do the harvesting by hand.

The crews start in the spring with sugar snap peas and snow peas. These are the green, edible pod snacks of springtime, the instant and raw delight for the ravenous. On the other hand, English peas, their legume contemporaries, may have a heartier texture but are tender with a delicate, sweet taste.

Throughout the summer the crew harvests green beans, yellow wax beans, and haricots verts, which are a special variety picked young, thin and tender green beans. Give them another week and they grow into full-size green beans.

Fresh, shelling beans bookend the busy season on the Island, with fava beans seventy-five days after their mid-May planting, and edamame-style soybeans and lima beans in August and September. Legumes span the seasons. Snap peas, for instance, are planted every week from May to September, with fifty days from seed to harvest.

Green Beans and Pasta Salad

1 lb. fresh cavatelli pasta, or other dry, shaped pasta

1 wedge lemon

½ lb. fresh green beans, stemmed, cut in 1½"–2" at an angle

1 pt. cherry or grape tomatoes, halved or quartered (see instructions for roasting note)

Sea salt and pepper

¼ c. sliced almonds, lightly toasted

4 oz. prepared Arugula or Sweet Pea Pesto (recipe, page 77)

Preheat oven to 350°.

Cook pasta according to package directions. If cooking fresh pasta, heat salted water to a boil; add pasta and lemon wedge. Cook 7–8 minutes; at the last 45 seconds, add the green beans. Immediately remove from heat and pour into colander, rinse thoroughly, and immerse colander in a bowl of ice water.

Meanwhile, prepare the tomatoes. For an additional boost of flavor you can roast the tomatoes (toss cut tomatoes with 1 tsp. olive oil and place on lined baking sheet, sprinkle with salt, place in oven while almonds are toasting, 10–12 minutes).

Sprinkle almonds with salt; toast until they turn honey-tan color. Remove from oven and cool 8–10 minutes.

Remove pasta and beans from water bath and let dry. In a bowl, combine pasta and beans with the tomatoes and pesto. Mix thoroughly. Taste and adjust seasonings if needed. Sprinkle with almonds before serving.

> **CHEF'S NOTE:** If roasting the tomatoes, skip the beans and chop up a few varieties of our patty pan squash. Roast until they begin to brown, along with the tomatoes, extra virgin olive oil, and salt.

CROP NOTES: *Any of our pole/bush bean varieties will be excellent used here.*

Quinoa and Pea Salad

SPECIAL EQUIPMENT: MEDIUM SAUCEPAN WITH LID / SERVINGS: 4

1 c. quinoa, dry

2 c. shelling peas

1 c. mango, diced

1 red bell pepper, diced

1 cucumber, diced

1 c. cherry tomatoes, halved

¼ c. olive oil

¼ tsp. salt

Ground pepper, to taste

2 c. water

8 c. mixed salad greens

Balsamic vinegar

1 avocado, diced (optional)

Recipe contributed by Vineyard Nutrition

Bring water to a boil in medium-covered pot. Add quinoa, bring back to a boil, cover, reduce heat to low, and cook for 20 minutes.

Prepare peas.

In a large bowl, combine olive oil, salt, pepper, mango, peas, bell pepper, cucumber, and tomatoes; mix.

Slowly stir in the quinoa and avocado, if using.

Serve over bed of mixed salad greens. Can be served hot or cold, with balsamic vinegar or low-sodium salad dressing.

Warm Green Bean Salad
with Feta, Olives, Almonds, and Lemon-Oregano Vinaigrette

3 Tbsp. plus ½ tsp. extra virgin olive oil

¼ medium red onion, peeled and sliced very thinly

Kosher salt

12 oz. green beans or a combination of green and yellow wax beans, trimmed

1 Tbsp. balsamic vinegar

1 scant tsp. fresh grated lemon zest

½ tsp. honey

Fresh ground black pepper

1 Tbsp. fresh oregano, chopped

1 Tbsp. Kalamata olives, pitted and chopped

1–2 Tbsp. finely crumbled feta cheese

1 Tbsp. toasted almonds, finely chopped

Recipe contributed by Susie Middleton, cookbook author and West Tisbury farmer, who notes, "Cook green or yellow wax beans just until you can bite through them (don't undercook or they'll be rubbery); dress while warm for the best flavor. The Greek-inspired flavors here are particularly nice with beans (and crunchy almonds add texture), but you could use your favorite homemade vinaigrette any day for a warm bean salad. Add cherry tomatoes and fresh corn for an all-American spin."

In small nonstick skillet, heat ½ tsp. olive oil over medium-high heat. Add red onion; cook, stirring, until the onion has just softened, about 2 minutes. Set aside.

Fill sauce pot half full with water and 2 tsp. kosher salt; bring to a boil. Arrange a few layers of dishtowels on a work surface to drain the beans. Add the beans to boiling water and begin timing. Boil until the beans are tender to the bite, but still green, 5–8 minutes. Test after 3 minutes; depending on the age of beans, there can be a wide range in cooking time.

Drain the beans or use tongs to lift them out of the water. Spread out on dishtowels to let excess moisture drain and evaporate, about 5 minutes.

Meanwhile, whisk together the remaining olive oil, vinegar, lemon zest, honey, ⅛ tsp. salt, and pinch of black pepper in small bowl. Add the oregano and olives. Whisk until combined.

Arrange the cooled beans on a platter or in a shallow bowl and drizzle with the dressing. Top with onion, cheese, and almond. Serve warm or at room temperature.

Green Bean Casserole

2 Tbsp. olive oil

1 bunch fresh green onions, 3–4 bulbs, cut in half, then across up to 3″ of stem

1 bulb fennel, cored, julienned

1 leek, white only, cut in half lengthwise, slice across ¼″

2 tsp. fresh thyme, finely chopped

1 tsp. sea salt, and more to taste

¼ tsp. black pepper, and more to taste

¼ tsp. nutmeg

⅛ tsp. lemon zest

Large pot boiling water

Squeeze of lemon juice

2 lb. green beans, trimmed, cut in 2″ pieces

1 c. sour cream

4 oz. fresh goat cheese

In skillet, heat oil. Add onions, fennel, leek, thyme, salt, pepper, nutmeg, and lemon zest. Sweat vegetables over low heat, 8–10 minutes.

Meanwhile, bring pot of water to boil with pinch of salt and a squeeze of lemon juice. Blanch green beans 1 minute. Remove with slotted spoon and place in ice-water bath to stop cooking. Strain, let dry.

As the beans dry, fold in the sour cream and goat cheese. Continue to mix until they are fully incorporated and the vegetables are fully coated. The green beans will be added and either tossed over heat to warm or tossed and set under a broiler for 3–5 minutes. If broiling, remove the skillet when the top of the vegetable mixture begins to brown.

Best served warm.

CROP NOTES: *Fresh green bean varieties harvested in season offer both a flavor profile as well as a wonderfully crisp texture. This recipe is a take on the classic green bean casserole with the intent of highlighting the qualities of the fresh bean.*

Country-Style Beans

SPECIAL EQUIPMENT: HEAVY SKILLET, ROASTING PAN / SERVINGS: 4

¼ lb. pork fat, cured, salted, raw, or smoked

¼ lb. bacon, cut into matchsticks

½ c. dried cranberry beans (cooked earlier)

15 oz. can cannellini beans, drained and rinsed

½ c. unsulfured molasses

1 Tbsp. dried mustard powder

¼ c. raw, unfiltered apple cider vinegar

Sea salt to taste

¼ tsp. black pepper

¼ tsp. allspice

If using dried beans, soak in 4 cups cold water over night. Rinse before use and cook in advance. If using canned beans, rinse thoroughly.

Heat oven to 250°.

Melt the pork fat in skillet, then render bacon at medium-low temperature until soft and bacon fat is translucent but not crisp.

Fold in remaining ingredients. Stir thoroughly while over the heat, bringing to a boil.

Place in a roasting pan and cover tightly with aluminum foil. Slow roast for three hours. See Sweet and Sour Country-Style Ribs (recipe, page 46) for easy preparation.

Hummus Theme and Variations

This is our base. It will keep in refrigerator up to 1 week.

One 15-oz. can chickpeas, or ½ c. dried chickpeas

1 Tbsp. Roasted Garlic, or 3 cloves (recipe, page 51)

2 Tbsp. tahini

2 Tbsp. lemon juice

1 tsp. sea salt, or to taste

¼ tsp. cumin

⅛ tsp. cayenne

¼ c. extra virgin olive oil

If using dried chickpeas, soak in cool water overnight, strain, cook in cool water until soft, drain, and let dry. If using canned chickpeas, drain, rinse, and let dry.

Place prepared chickpeas in food processor; pulse until coarsely chopped. Add remaining ingredients except oil; pulse to incorporate. Slowly drizzle in oil to create smooth texture.

Variations: Common additions to incorporate with chickpeas:

Carrot or butternut squash: 2 carrots or 1 cup squash, drizzle with ½ tsp. extra virgin olive oil and ½ tsp. curry powder, roast at 375° for 30 minutes, until soft and slightly caramelized ⊙ Sweet peas: ½ cup shelled ⊙ Roasted tomatoes: ½ cup oven roasted, tossed in extra virgin olive oil, roast at 375°, 25–30 minutes ⊙ Asparagus: ½ bunch, mid-stalk to tip, blanched or roasted ⊙ Roasted red peppers: roast pepper whole, drizzled with olive oil, and with stem, skin, and seeds removed.

CHEF'S NOTE: Since canned beans can have elevated sodium levels, choose a low- or no-salt added variety. This will allow better adjustment of salt with each variation.

CROP NOTES: *Hummus has become a mainstay in our prepared-foods refrigerator. This base recipe is designed to be very adaptable; incorporate early-season crops such as asparagus and peas through to autumn's bounty of squash and roots. The amount of oil will vary depending on the moisture content of each crop. Simply begin with ¼ cup and adapt accordingly. Be bold and explore arugula, herbs, eggplant—roasted or raw. The combinations will change throughout the year.*

Quinoa Cranberry Bean Pilaf

SPECIAL EQUIPMENT: 6-QT. SAUCEPAN, BAKING SHEET / SERVINGS: 4 GENEROUS

½ c. dried cranberry beans

5 ¼ qt. cool water

1 tsp. sea salt, divided

2 Tbsp. extra virgin olive oil, divided

1 c. dried golden quinoa

1 butternut squash, peeled, seeded, medium dice

4 ears corn, kernelled

1 tsp. smoked paprika

1 tsp. cumin

2 Tbsp. butter

1 medium-large onion, medium dice

2 carrots, medium dice

2 ribs celery, medium dice

1 leek, white only, cut lengthwise, then across

1 Tbsp. fresh thyme, finely minced

1 tsp. sage, freshly chopped

½ tsp. black pepper

1 Tbsp. fresh miso, dissolved in 2 Tbsp. warm water

Substitute brown rice or farro for quinoa. A 15-oz. can of beans equals ½ cup dried beans. Any type of squash or pumpkin may be used in place of butternut.

Soak the cranberry beans in 3 cups cool water overnight. The next day, drain and rinse beans. Place beans in 6-qt. saucepan with 3 qts. cool water; bring to boil, simmer 25–28 minutes.

Preheat oven to 375°.

In 4-qt. saucepan, bring 2 ¼ cups cool water, ¼ tsp. sea salt, and ½ tsp. olive oil to a boil. Add quinoa; stir and cover, reduce heat, simmer 20–22 minutes.

Place butternut squash and corn in bowl. Add 1 Tbsp. olive oil, paprika, and cumin; toss to coat squash and corn. Lay squash and corn out on lined baking sheet; bake 20–25 minutes, until squash is soft.

In large pot, add remaining oil and butter; melt over medium heat. Add onions, carrots, celery, leek, and thyme; cook 12–15 minutes until onion is completely soft. Add sage, salt, and pepper; stir and continue to cook. Fold in beans, quinoa, squash, corn and miso.

CHEF'S NOTE: Cranberry beans are high in nutritional value and make a great addition to a number of dishes. They get their name from the appearance of their pods, which are often red or pink. The beans themselves are usually white or cream in color with deep red specks, which typically disappear as they darken during cooking.

CROP NOTES: This is a great stuffing for roasted sugar pumpkin or Long Island Cheese pumpkin. Split, seed, and roast the pumpkin ahead of time until flesh is soft and can easily pull from the skin. Add the pilaf mixture, then roast an additional 30 minutes.

Four Bean Salad

One 15-oz. can each: chickpeas, black, and kidney beans, or ½ c. dry beans of each, cooked earlier

4 Tbsp. extra virgin olive oil

1 Tbsp. Dijon mustard

1 Tbsp. raw, unfiltered apple cider vinegar

1 Tbsp. dill, finely minced

½ tsp. hot sauce (we recommend our vinegar basic roasted poblano sauce)

¼ tsp. lemon zest

½–1 tsp. sea salt, varies based on sodium level of canned product

⅛ tsp. black pepper

4 medium carrots, shredded

1 red onion, finely diced

½ lb. green beans cut in half if small, or 2″ pieces if large

This recipe can be scaled back to use just one of the three beans in dry or canned form, green beans remaining the constant. We will do a large batch of this recipe for a summer picnic.

Standard canned beans, 15-oz. can yields approximately 1½ lb. ready-to-go beans.

If substituting dried beans, use ½ cup dry beans, which soaked overnight and cooked will yield the equivalent of the canned beans.

The three beans we prefer are chickpeas, black beans, and kidney beans, but many varieties would be a fine substitute. All beans soak and cook at different rates, which can become cumbersome.

In bowl, whisk oil, mustard, vinegar, dill, hot sauce, lemon zest, salt, and pepper until fully combined. Add carrots, red onions, green beans, and beans; mix thoroughly.

This can be served immediately at room temperature or refrigerated and served the next day. Will remain fine chilled up to 5 days.

> **CHEF'S NOTE:** If using canned beans, drain and rinse in colander. If using dry beans, soak overnight and cook until tender. After cooking, strain beans and place in a cold-water bath to stop cooking. Strain, let dry, and set aside.

CROP NOTES: Green beans: *At the height of the season, beans are tender enough to be used fresh instead of blanching. Salad can be marinated overnight, and there is no need for any cooking of green beans. Later in the harvest as beans get larger, we recommend blanching. In 6-qt. pot, bring 2 qts. water to a boil with squeeze of fresh lemon juice and pinch of sea salt. Immerse for no more than 30 seconds; remove immediately and place in ice-water bath. When cooled, strain and pat dry.*

Farm Food ✳ III

Warm Chickpea Salad

SPECIAL EQUIPMENT: MEDIUM SIZED SAUTÉ PAN / SERVINGS: 4

½ c. dried chickpeas soaked overnight in 4 c. cold water over night (or use one 15-oz. can)

2 eggplant, medium, ½" dice

2¼ tsp. sea salt, divided

¼ c. olive oil, divided

1 onion, medium, ½" dice

2 bell peppers, stem, seeds, and pith removed, ½" dice

2 summer squash, small, ½" dice

1 sprig rosemary, stemmed, finely minced, divided

½ tsp. ground cumin

¼ tsp. dried chili flakes

⅛ tsp. ground cloves

4 tomatoes, skin and seeds intact, ½" dice

1 Tbsp. raw, unfiltered apple cider vinegar

2 sprigs basil, 10–12 leaves, rolled and cut into fine ribbons

If using dried chickpeas, rinse and cook at a simmer for 1 hour or until done.

Preheat oven to 375°.

Place diced eggplant in non-reactive bowl and toss with 2 tsp. salt. Let sit for 45 minutes to 1 hour. Press the eggplant to extract excess moisture.

Place on a lined sheet pan. Drizzle with 2 Tbsp. olive oil, place in oven, and roast for 25 minutes or until nicely caramelized.

Bring a sauté pan up to temperature at medium heat. Heat 2 Tbsp. olive oil in pan, and add the onions. Sauté for 6–8 minutes or until soft but not browned. Add bell peppers and squash for another 3–5 minutes.

Add ½ of minced rosemary, cumin, chili flakes, and cloves to the mixture and cook for 3–5 minutes.

Add tomatoes, chickpeas, cooked eggplant, and vinegar and reduce to low heat and stir and simmer for 10-12 minutes.

Put ingredients in a serving dish and sprinkle remaining rosemary and basil over the top.

CROP NOTES: Tomatoes: *Choose firm rather than overripe tomatoes for this recipe.*

THE FARM STAND: DEBBIE'S TERRITORY

In many ways, the farm stand is the very center of life at the farm. The stand bustles with Island residents and visitors, many carrying a coffee and fresh-baked muffin, a fresh juice or lunch from the salad bar, or toting the makings of a cookout.

Outside are the flower bunchers floating between buckets of fresh-cut flowers, plucking one of these, several of those, and just a touch of that to create a unique bouquet. They seem to do it effortlessly.

Inside, it's all color, texture, and height.

These are the guiding principles of design for Debbie Athearn, who is the heart and mind behind the stand and has been since the family sold their first crop under a sun umbrella on the side of the road almost forty years ago. The front table is always a showcase of what is ripe and ready for harvest. It changes daily, with combinations of asparagus, radishes, Asian greens, and herbs in the spring; blueberries, peaches, kale, and peppers in July; tomatoes, squash, and beans in September. It consistently demonstrates Debbie's eye for aesthetics and an understanding that you eat first with your eyes, then with your mouth.

"You want different colors. If you have beets and radishes side by side, they kind of blend together. You want to see something separating that color," says Debbie. "I always like to have the really ruffly cut greens paired up besides something that's more rigid and straight. And I'm always talking about height."

Debbie encourages her staff to get creative. "This isn't just selling vegetables. You get to use your creative side, to have fun with this, and just make it pop!" she tells them.

The staff answers customers' questions: *Do you have farm strawberries now? What do I do with kohlrabi?* But so do the colorful, hand-drawn signs that provide history, nutritional facts, culinary tips, and other information that normally only the farmers would be privy to: the basil is sold as loose leaves right now because of downy mildew, or "last peppers of the season!"

A couple of years earlier Debbie and her staff decided to make signs on the computer, to save time on handwriting them. "We had so many people comment, "Where are your beautiful hand-made signs? They noticed it," Debbie exclaims.

It's like what her husband, Jim, says: "The customers train us more than we train them." The signs continue to be handwritten, hand-drawn, and as colorful as ever.

PUMPKINS & WINTER SQUASH
Late Harvests, Great Food

Just before autumn officially arrives, the lawn in front of the farm stand bursts ablaze. Pumpkins circle the trees, lay on the grass, and line the railing of the back porch. Fall has come to Morning Glory, and the farm glows orange.

"Winter squash harvest marks the beginning of the next season," says Ethan Valenti, field crew manager at Morning Glory. Though crowds are thinner, the crew is also smaller, and the fast pace of work continues. But winter squash harvest is undeniably playful.

Valenti picks up a pumpkin, hoists it above his right shoulder, and tosses it high into the air. It lands on the ground with a splat, bursting into a thousand pieces.

That was a rotten one, not to be added to the bin of salable pumpkins.

The crew on the ground takes turns picking up winter squash and throwing them to their coworkers standing in the bed of a moving truck. They catch the squash and add them carefully to enormous cardboard bins. In the summertime, these bins hold watermelons. Come fall, they are loaded with tons of winter squash of all kinds. The field crew will harvest about nineteen thousand pounds of pumpkins and tons more of butternut, spaghetti, acorn, sunshine, delicata, sweet dumpling, hubbard, and decorative gourds.

Unlike summer squash, winter squash are harvested at full maturity.

The pumpkins are bright orange. Acorn squash have a defined yellow spot where they were resting on the ground. The plant tendril closest to the squash has died back, and the sugar content, measured by the Athearns with a device called a refractometer, is high enough. But the rinds are still soft and easily punctured, and the flavor can benefit from additional ripening, away from the threats of frost and deer.

Immediately after harvest, the crew transfers the squash into the greenhouse to cure for two weeks. Careful handling is key: any bruises made to the tender squash at this point will cause them to rot more quickly. It is during this period of curing that the rinds harden, enabling squash to last into the wintertime. The starches continue to convert to sugars, and the squash grow sweeter and more flavorful.

The hard rind on winter squash make it difficult to open. Obviously, a large sharp knife and lots of leverage is one way to go. But another option, according to a squash-loving home cook, is to nuke the squash for a few minutes in the microwave, making it softer and easier to slice in half. She uses this trick for sugar pumpkins in particular and says it has saved her hands from many cuts.

Roast Dumpling Squash or "Raptor Claws"

2 sweet dumpling squash

1 Tbsp. butter or extra virgin olive oil

1 tsp. total "warm" spices, any combo: cinnamon, clove, ginger, or nutmeg

¼ tsp. sea salt

⅛ tsp. black pepper

1 Tbsp. maple syrup

Preheat oven to 350°.

To prepare squash, place stem end down on a cutting surface and cut squash in half across, going along the indentations. With a large spoon, scoop out seeds and membrane. Continue cutting at every indentation, ending up with one-inch crescent shape pieces.

Melt butter in a small pan over low heat; add spices, salt, and pepper. Cook, stirring constantly, 2 minutes, allowing spices to flavor the butter.

Place the squash in a large mixing bowl; pour spiced butter and maple syrup over squash. Toss to fully coat. Place squash on lined baking sheet, bake 25–28 minutes.

CHEF'S NOTE: This recipe was developed for our school lunch program here on Martha's Vineyard. The shape of the cut squash resembles raptor claws.

Spicy Pork and Butternut Soup

with Kale and Cranberry Beans

SPECIAL EQUIPMENT: 6-QT. SAUCEPAN WITH LID / YIELD: 3 QTS.

1 Tbsp. olive oil

1 lb. pork, cubed (pork shoulder works best)

1 tsp. sea salt

¼ tsp. black pepper

2 medium or 1 large white onion, diced

3 cloves garlic, minced

1 fresh chili pepper, jalapeno or cayenne, stemmed, seeded, and minced

2 sprigs thyme, stemmed, finely minced

1 sprig rosemary, stemmed, finely minced

2 qts. stock, beef or pork, chicken for a lighter soup

½ lb. cranberry beans, soaked overnight and previously cooked, or one 15-oz. can cannellini or pinto beans, drained and rinsed

1 butternut squash, peeled, seeded, medium dice

1 bunch kale, 8–-10 leaves, stemmed, torn into bite-sized pieces

Recipe contributed by Chloe Nelson

Heat oil in 6-qt. saucepan. Toss diced pork with salt and pepper; add to pan, browning pork uniformly. Remove with slotted spoon, allowing oil and pork fat to remain in pan. At medium to medium-high heat, add onion, garlic, and chili pepper. Cook 5–8 minutes, stirring occasionally, until onions are soft. Add herbs and stir.

Add cooked pork, stock, and beans. Boil. Reduce heat to medium-low, cover, and cook 40 minutes, until beans are tender.

Add squash, simmering 15–20 minutes until squash is soft. Add kale, return to boiling, cover. Turn off heat and let soup rest, covered, 5–8 minutes.

Roasted Acorn Squash with Cranberry Butter

SPECIAL EQUIPMENT: SHALLOW BAKING DISH, FOOD PROCESSOR / SERVINGS: 2–4

2 acorn squash

Water

½ c. cranberries

4 Tbsp. butter, ½ stick

1 Tbsp. sage, stemmed and chopped

½ tsp. sea salt

⅛ tsp. black pepper

Dash hot sauce

⅛ tsp. nutmeg

¼ tsp. orange zest

Preheat oven to 375°.

Cut squashes in half. Use large spoon to scoop out seeds and membrane. Set in shallow baking pan. Pour in water to come ½″ up the side of squash.

Add cranberries to food processor; pulse until cranberries start to break up. Add butter, sage, salt, pepper, hot sauce, nutmeg, and orange zest, continue to pulse until incorporated. Spoon butter mixture into 4 equal quantities and place in the bowl of squash.

Bake 45 minutes, spinning the pan around once. The cut surface of squash should be caramelized, a rich golden brown, and the squash itself should be soft to the touch around the outside.

Butternut Squash, Kale, and Corn

½ lb. kale, leaves stripped off stems, chopped into bite-size pieces (about 5–6 c.)

3–4 c. water

1 Tbsp. olive oil

1 Tbsp. butter

1 small butternut squash, peeled and cut into ½–¾-inch dice (3–4 c.)

1½ c. corn kernels, 2 ears

⅛ tsp. cayenne

¼ tsp. cumin

½ tsp. kosher salt, plus more to taste

Freshly ground black pepper

1 lime, quartered

Recipe contributed by cookbook author and chef Catherine Walthers, who notes, "I found a winning combination for kale when the farm corn was still around and fall butternut squash came in, accented with cayenne, cumin and fresh lime." (Her next cookbook is Kale, Glorious Kale *coming out in the fall of 2014.)*

In large skillet with lid, bring 3–4 cups water to a boil. Add the kale; cover and cook over high heat, stirring occasionally, until tender, 5–7 minutes. Drain in a colander, shaking a few times to release steam and stop the cooking.

Dry the skillet; add the butter and olive oil over medium heat. Add the butternut squash and sauté, stirring occasionally, until lightly browned and cooked without falling apart, about 15 minutes (the pan should be large enough to fit the squash in a single layer). Add the corn, cayenne, cumin, salt, and pepper. Cook 4–5 minutes, until corn is cooked.

When ready to serve, add the kale and stir gently to warm. Add salt to taste. Squeeze lime into the dish, or allow people to squeeze their own.

Brussels Sprouts with Bacon

1 lb. Brussels sprouts, stemmed and halved

¼ lb. bacon, cut into matchsticks

½ tsp. mustard seed, or 1 tsp. coarse Dijon mustard

¼ tsp. anise seed

1 leek, white only, cut in half, then across into thin strips

1 onion, cut in half, finely julienned

¼ tsp. sea salt

1 pinch black pepper

1 tsp. lemon juice

Brussels sprouts can be prepared in a few ways. Oven roasted will give them a more caramelized look and earthy flavor. For a brighter color and more simple flavor, blanch in boiling water for 30 seconds, and immediately place in a cold water bath. Then dry in a colander and set aside.

In skillet, render the bacon. When bacon is just beginning to crisp, remove from pan with slotted spoon, keeping the fat drippings in pan. Add the mustard seed and anise seeds to pan. Stir around until fully coated with fat. Add leek, onion, salt, and pepper.

Cook until onion and leek are completely soft, about 10 minutes. Reintroduce the bacon and add the lemon juice. Fold in the Brussels sprouts and cook over medium heat for 5 minutes.

Roasted Pumpkin or Squash Soup

SPECIAL EQUIPMENT: BAKING PAN, 6-QT. SAUCEPAN, BLENDER OR IMMERSION BLENDER / SERVINGS: 4–6

6–8 lb. squash, 2 butternut or
  2 pie pumpkins

Water

2 Tbsp. butter

2 Tbsp. extra virgin olive oil

1 Tbsp. sage leaf, finely minced

1 tsp. pie spice, or any
  combination of cinnamon,
  ginger, clove, or allspice

2 medium white onions, medium
  dice

4 carrots, medium dice

1 leek, white only, medium dice

2 ribs celery, medium dice

¼ tsp. orange zest

1 Tbsp. Morning Glory's Mellow
  Yellow chili sauce

2 qts. commercial or homemade
  vegetable stock

1 c. heavy cream, optional

Preheat oven to 375°.

Wash squash. Cut in half, and with large spoon scoop out seeds and membrane. Reserve pumpkin seeds (see recipe, page 128).

Invert the squash onto a lined baking sheet. Pour enough water into pan to come up to ½″ of the side of the squash. Bake 45 minutes to 1 hour, until flesh gives to the touch. Let cool, peel away skins, set aside. There is no need to puree at this point.

Meanwhile, melt butter and oil in 6-qt. saucepan over medium heat. Add sage, pie spice, and vegetables; cook 10–12 minutes, until onions are soft. Do not let them brown. If they do begin to brown, remove pan from burner, reduce heat, and return to heat after 15 seconds.

Once onions are soft, add zest, hot sauce, vegetable stock, and squash. Stir to combine, increase heat to medium–high heat, and bring to a boil. Reduce heat and simmer 15–20 minutes.

Using immersion blender, puree soup until smooth. Use caution when pureeing hot soup in blender. Start by pulsing to check the pressure.

If using cream, drizzle in. Cream adds a richer, smoother flavor.

PEPPERS: SWEET OR HOT, PACKED WITH FLAVOR

The hot peppers are small and colorful, mixed together in a basket in the farm stand. They are red, yellow, and green. They are round cherry bombs, long and curvy cayennes, crinkly habaneros, or smooth jalapenos. There are a handful or more of different varieties of varying heat, which change from year to year depending on what the market demands and what varieties have proven themselves to grow well.

Beside the hot peppers are the large, mildly hot peppers such as the forest-green poblano and the anaheim pepper. These peppers, like the sweet Italian fryer, come to a single point at the bottom and are therefore called single-lobed peppers. Oftentimes, the sweet fryers are mistaken for hot peppers because of their shape,

Finally, there are the bell peppers, with three or four lobes, that are not spicy but still "peppery" in flavor. The purple bell peppers are juicy and thin-walled, while the red, yellow, and orange bell peppers are thicker walled, which makes them great for roasting. Green peppers are red, yellow, or orange peppers picked under ripe.

"Fall is the season for peppers. Red peppers taste really sweet in September and October. They're at their best then," says Simon Athearn.

Pork-Stuffed Cabbage or Peppers

SPECIAL EQUIPMENT: 6-QT. SAUCEPAN WITH LID, HEAVY-BOTTOM SKILLET, 9X13-INCH PAN / SERVINGS: 4–6

2¼ c. water

1 c. short-grain brown rice

3 tsp. sea salt, divided

8 large outer cabbage leaves or 4 medium-large bell peppers, halved

1 lb. loose pork sausage, breakfast, sweet or hot

2 Tbsp. extra virgin olive oil, divided

1 onion, medium dice

2 ribs celery, medium dice

1 leek, white only, medium dice

½ bulb fennel, cored, medium dice, optional

1 tsp. fennel seed

1 Tbsp. fresh sage, finely minced

1 tsp. thyme leaves, finely minced

1 bunch greens, collards, Swiss chard, or kale, stemmed, cut into thin ribbons

1 tsp. hot sauce

Tomato sauce or Deb's Garden Special (recipe, page 191)

Boil water, rice, and 1 tsp. salt in 6-qt. saucepan, cover, reduce heat, and simmer 40–45 minutes until all water is absorbed.

Meanwhile, if using cabbage, bring 2 qts. water and 1 tsp. salt to a boil. Using long tongs, place cabbage, one leaf at a time, in boiling water, fully immersed, 10 seconds. Remove and place in bowl of ice water. After all 8 leaves have been blanched, strain and pat dry each leaf. Set aside.

In heavy-bottom skillet over medium-high heat, brown sausage, stirring to mix and crumble into small pieces. Cook 7–8 minutes until rendered and brown. Remove sausage with slotted spoon, leaving drippings in pan.

Add 1 Tbsp. oil to pork fat; add onions, celery, leek, fennel, fennel seeds, and fresh herbs. Cook over medium-high heat 10 minutes, until vegetables are soft. Combine sausage and vegetables in large bowl.

Add remaining oil to pan and sauté greens over medium-high heat, until limp. Chard will take 3 minutes, "pre-frost" collards will take 5 minutes, and "post-frost" collards or kale will take 6–8 minutes.

Remove greens from pan and add to bowl of sausage and vegetables. Pour the hot sauce over the top and add the rice. Mix thoroughly. Preheat oven to 350°. Line 9x13-inch baking pan with sauce.

If using cabbage, place a leaf on work surface, stem side toward edge. Place ½ cup sausage filling into leaf, filling up ⅓ of the leaf. Roll stem end up over mixture. Fold each side in toward middle, meeting in middle or overlapping. Continue to roll cabbage toward back of work surface, until it reaches leaf tip. Place seam side down in prepared pan.

If using peppers, place ¾–1 cup mixture in pepper halves, mounding over the edge of pepper about 2–3″. Place in prepared pan.

Bake 45 minutes.

Roasted Pumpkin Seeds

Seeds from pumpkin

1 tsp. olive oil

Pinch sea salt

Pinch cumin, optional

Pinch black pepper, optional

Preheat oven to 375°.

The easiest way to remove the seeds from the membrane is to soak in warm water. Seeds should pull away easier. Dry seeds, toss in bowl with olive oil, salt, and spices, if using.

Spread on lined baking sheet. Roast with squash 15–18 minutes.

Garnish soup with roasted seeds.

Oven-Fried Delicata Squash Rings

4 delicata squash

2 Tbsp. butter, melted

1 Tbsp. olive oil

Salt and pepper to taste

1 Tbsp. chopped fresh thyme

Recipe contributed by Jan Pogue of Edgartown

Preheat oven to 425°.

Have on hand two large rimmed baking sheets.

With a long paring knife, cut the squash into ½˝-thick rounds. Then cut around the centers of the rounds to remove the seeds.

Place the squash on a baking sheet. (Covering the sheets with non-stick aluminum foil will speed cleanup.) Pour the butter and the olive oil over the rings. Turn the rings so they're coated on both sides. Sprinkle with salt and pepper.

Arrange the rings so that they do not overlap. Bake for 20–30 minutes until they are golden brown and tender. (No need to turn.)

Stack the rings on a platter, sprinkle with a little more salt and thyme, and serve at once.

> **CHEF'S NOTE:** Love those breaded French-fried onion rings but know how bad they are for you? Try these as a delicious alternative.

Braised Red Cabbage and Farro

SPECIAL EQUIPMENT: 6-QT. SAUCEPAN, HEAVY-BOTTOM SKILLET / SERVINGS: 4

1 c. pearled farro

1½ c. water

1 pinch sea salt

1 half head red cabbage

2 Tbsp. extra virgin olive oil

1 tsp. caraway seed

1 Tbsp. minced anise hyssop
(substitute ½ tsp. fennel seed)

1 leek, white only, julienned

4 pearl onions, or spring onions,
peeled and quartered

2 Tbsp. orange juice or apple cider

1 Tbsp. raw, unfiltered apple cider
vinegar

1 Tbsp. coarse mustard

Over medium heat, toast farro 3–5 minutes in 6-qt. saucepan. Add water and salt. Bring to a boil, then simmer 15 minutes. Pour into a colander to drain excess liquid; set aside.

Meanwhile, core the cabbage, cut across in ¼″ ribbons, and halve.

In heavy-bottom skillet, over medium heat, heat oil, caraway and anise or fennel seeds, leeks, and quartered pearl onion. Cook 8–12 minutes or until onions are completely soft, borderline translucent, but no color.

Add red cabbage, anise hyssop or fennel seed, orange juice or cider, and apple cider vinegar. Mix to coat cabbage; cook 15–18 minutes. Fold in mustard and farro to incorporate.

CROP NOTES: *The red cabbage is selected here primarily for its color. Green cabbage, varieties of kale, collards—all would work well here. Likewise, the pearl onions have many substitutes; we just like the size and shape. Freshly harvested cabbage will release liquid as it cooks, whereas cold storage heads may require a few tablespoons of water while cooking to avoid sticking to the pan.*

ROOT VEGETABLES
Treasure Hunting

Root vegetables, like potatoes, beets, carrots, parsnips, and turnips, are often neither beautiful in the fields nor interesting to look at in the kitchen. They can be nubby and misshapen, with hairy roots and dull colors.

But harvesting them—and using them—is where the mundane meets the miraculous, where the rituals of labor generate the miracles of growing food.

You tug on the green foliage of a potato plant, and what emerges is not just one potato, but four, six, eight potatoes, dangling from a web of roots. You dig your hands into the cool soil, feeling for any potato that eluded you. In the subterranean search, your hands become your eyes.

"It's like finding gold," says Chris Nolan of the field crew, "especially with the Yukon golds, because they kind of look like gold."

"It's a discovery," says Jim Athearn. "You pull up a plant . . . potatoes! And then you pull up another plant . . . wow, potatoes! And you can be surprised every time."

To grow a potato, you plant a potato. In the spring, the Athearns order seed potatoes from a farm in Maine: a single seed potato is cut into two, four, or six pieces, if it is really big. "But that's artful cutting," says Jim. The seed pieces should be blocky, the size of a hen's egg, and with at least two eyes. Those are the Morning Glory guidelines. An eye, also called a bud, is what produces the sprout.

Two acres of potatoes are planted in a day and a half's time, using a potato-planting machine that funnels the seeds into trenches in the ground and covers them back up with soil. A single planting yields roughly twenty thousand pounds of potatoes, harvested from late spring, throughout the summer, and into the fall.

But only new potatoes are harvested by hand. Their skins are too thin, and their flesh too delicate, to harvest by machine. They are immature tubers—low in starch, moist, and unlike full-grown potatoes, quickly perishable.

Come midsummer, and the foliage of the potato vine starts to die back. Photosynthesis slows and then comes to a halt, as the greens whither away in the heat. The potatoes have bulked up to their maximum size. They continue to sit in the ground, where their skins firm up, and they become suitable for long storage periods. These potatoes are starchy and dense. They thicken soups and stews, and lend a creaminess that, at Morning Glory, sometimes replaces dairy in a soup.

The potatoes are sold by weight, and new potatoes naturally cost more than large ones. Come fall, the cost of potatoes falls to less than a dollar per pound. They will store for two to three months without sprouting, or even longer if you keep them in a cool place. No matter where you keep them, make sure it's dark.

PAEAN TO THE POTATO

THE FOLLOWING IS AN EXCERPT FROM AN ESSAY WRITTEN BY ROBYN ATHEARN,
WIFE OF SIMON, AFTER A DAY OF POTATO HARVEST AT MORNING GLORY:

There was just something about the magic of the work that day. I had been harvesting for hours by hand. My brother worked ahead of me in the row, loosening the soil with a spade fork. I, moving on my knees, would follow behind him, digging down deep into the earth with my hands feeling for potatoes and sifting them up through the dirt. Everyone says it, but it is exactly like digging for treasure. My arms from my fingertips to my shoulders were covered with beautiful, rich soil.

Near the end of the day as I sipped water by the tailgate, I took the whole scene in. A profound sense of peace came over me as I realized that every single thing we need is right here, literally, every single thing, right here, right under our feet. All we have to do is work with it a little.

Duck Fat Roasted Potatoes

2 lb. assorted potatoes: fingerlings, red, small sweet, small russet, Peruvian blue

2 Tbsp. rendered duck fat

1 Tbsp. rosemary, finely minced, or 1 sprig stemmed and minced

½ tsp. caraway seed

½ tsp. salt

¼ tsp. black pepper

Preheat oven to 400°.

Thoroughly wash and dry potatoes. Cut in half or quarters depending on size of potatoes.

In small saucepan, melt rendered duck fat. In bowl, toss together the potatoes, melted fat, and herbs and seasonings. Spread onto lined baking sheet, scraping bowl with rubber spatula to get all the fat. Roast potatoes 45 minutes, stirring twice during baking time, after 25 minutes and again at 35 minutes. Cut sides should be caramelized to a rich brown and insides soft.

Alternatively, rendered pork fat can be used in place of duck fat. Duck fat helps level the roasting time of the various potato types and has a richer flavor.

CHEF'S NOTE: Although Morning Glory does not sell rendered duck fat, you can usually buy it at any specialty food store.

Pickled Hakurei Turnips

6–8 bunches Hakurei and scarlet turnips

1 Tbsp. salt

1 recipe basic pickling brine (recipe, page 73)

½ tsp. turmeric

1 quarter size slice fresh ginger

Always check safe canning methods at the National Center for Home Food Preservation, www.nchfp.uga.edu

Wash turnips. Remove stem ends and stalks; leave skins on. Turnips may be sliced or shredded. If shredding, add 2 more bunches to reach proper yield. Salt turnips, refrigerate 30–60 minutes, remove and pat dry.

In a stainless steel pot, bring brine, turmeric, and ginger to a full rolling boil. Pour hot brine over turnips. Can be jarred immediately, following any established canning procedures.

Alternatively, let cool, place in sterilized jars, cover with appropriate lid, and refrigerate. The turnips will last for an extended period of time refrigerated.

CROP NOTES: *The white, golf-ball-sized spring turnips are abundant throughout most of our season. We often combine scarlet turnips and various varieties of radish to this brine. The colors of any addition will taint the Hakurei, turning it from the yellow hue assumed from the turmeric to a rose or salmon. The flavor will not, however, be dramatically altered. We keep properly jarred turnips for our salads for a year. Although safe, they begin to loose brightness of flavor.*

Roasted Cape White Turnips
with Yukon Gold potatoes

SPECIAL EQUPMENT: ROASTING PAN / SERVINGS: 4–6

2 Tbsp. extra virgin olive oil

2 lb. Cape White turnips, peeled, cut in half, sliced ¼″ across

1 lb. Yukon Gold potatoes, skin on, cut in half, sliced ½″ across

1 onion, cut in half, sliced ¼″ across

1 sprig rosemary, finely minced

¼ lb. bacon, cut ½″ slices

½ tsp. sea salt

¼ tsp. black pepper

½ tsp. mustard seed

Preheat oven to 425°.

Drizzle oil evenly over roasting pan. Mix in vegetables, rosemary, and bacon. Sprinkle with salt, pepper, and mustard seed.

Roast 40 minutes. After 20 minutes and every 10 minutes after, stir vegetables.

CROP NOTES: *Cape Whites are a wonderfully sweet turnip variety. They caramelize well when roasted. When fresh, the skins can be scrubbed clean and left intact. If used as a storage vegetable, peeling would be beneficial.*

Cured Pork Belly and Parsnips

SPECIAL EQUIPMENT: ROASTING PAN, HEAVY-BOTTOM SKILLET / SERVINGS: 4–6

2 lb. parsnips

2 Tbsp. extra virgin olive oil

½ tsp. ground coriander

½ tsp. sea salt

¼ tsp. black pepper

½ lb. cured pork belly, or smoked bacon

1 large, or 2 medium onions, medium diced

2 ribs celery, medium diced

1 leek, white only, medium diced

1 tsp. mustard seed

½ tsp. caraway seed

1 scant Tbsp. winter savory, stemmed and chopped, about 2 sprigs

2 Tbsp. raw, unfiltered apple cider vinegar

1 Tbsp. molasses

Preheat oven to 400°.

Cut parsnips lengthwise (if peeling, do so first), then across at an angle for 1½ to 2-inch pieces. Toss with oil, coriander, salt and pepper. Place into roasting pan; roast for 45 minutes or until exterior of parsnips caramelizes to a golden brown color and the interior is soft to the touch. Remove from oven.

Meanwhile, medium dice, or slice across into matchsticks, the pork belly. Render in a heavy-bottom skillet at medium-low heat until just starting to crisp. Remove meat from pan with slotted spoon, retaining drippings in pan.

Increase heat to medium; add onion, celery, leek, seeds, and herbs. Cook until vegetables are soft, 10–12 minutes. Add vinegar and drizzle molasses; stir to incorporate. Remove from heat.

Add pork and vegetables to the roasting pan with the parsnips. Mix together and return to oven for 5–7 minutes.

Serve warm.

> **CHEF'S NOTE:** The benefit of patience in using late harvest wintered or cellared parsnips is the beautiful aroma and natural sweetness that enhances the flavor. The need for added sugars, as in the molasses in this recipe, becomes less over time. Rosemary or thyme would be a fine alternative to the winter savory.

CROP NOTES: Parsnips: *Much like Brussels sprouts, parsnips are received in the fall with a great degree of anticipation. First of the season, harvested in mid- to late fall, are moist with a mild flavor. Washed well, the skins can remain. As the root cures in storage, it loses a bit of its moisture, and the skins are better removed.*

Potato and Green Bean Salad

1 lb. new red potatoes

Water

1 tsp. white vinegar, or lemon juice

½ lb. green beans, or haricot vertes, stemmed and cut at an angle 2½–3″

¼ lb. smoked bacon or cured pork belly

½ bulb fennel, cored and sliced across in ¼″ slices

½ c. Pickled Red Onion, coarsely chopped (recipe, page 142)

1 tsp. finely chopped dill

¼ c. olive oil

2 tsp. whole grain mustard

2 tsp. raw, unfiltered apple cider vinegar

⅛ tsp. hot sauce

½ tsp. sea salt

⅛ tsp. black pepper

If the new potatoes are smaller in diameter than a quarter, use whole. Otherwise cut in half or quarters and place in 6-qt. saucepan, covering with water to an inch over the potatoes. Bring to a boil, reduce to a simmer, and cook 20–22 minutes or until potatoes are tender but not soft. Add white vinegar and beans; cook an additional 45 seconds to 1 minute. Strain and place in ice water bath until cool. Remove and shake dry.

Meanwhile, in skillet over medium heat, render bacon until it begins to brown, 8–10 minutes. Add fennel; cook 2 minutes. Place potatoes, green beans, bacon, fennel, red onion, and dill into a large bowl.

Combine oil, mustard, cider vinegar, hot sauce, salt, and pepper in a small bowl. Whisk until thoroughly combined. Drizzle over potato mixture and stir to incorporate. Serve while bacon is still warm.

> **CHEF'S NOTE:** Green beans can certainly be blanched separately, but with so little starch in the water, piggybacking for the last minutes seems appropriate. Cooking the potatoes slowly will allow them to keep their shape.

CROP NOTES: Potatoes: *The small, early-season potato, when fresh, offers a bright potato flavor with a clean, low-starch texture. Any of our other potato varieties can be used here, but most will begin to fall apart or release starch, leading to a "gummy" texture—not a bad thing, just a different result.*

Pickled Red Onions

Always check safe canning methods at the National Center for Home Food Preservation, www.nchfp.uga.edu

2 lb. red onions, 4 medium

2 c. white vinegar

1 tsp. sea salt

1 Tbsp. pickling spices, pre-made or store-bought, or any combination of: black pepper, coriander, fennel, caraway seeds, anise, celery seeds, mustard seeds

¼ c. sugar

Note: We like to make this ahead of time and use it as a staple in our salad bar and prepared salads.

Stem and peel onions. Finely slice with food processor or mandolin.

Whisk together vinegar, salt, spices, and sugar. Place onions in jars; pour room-temperature vinegar mixture over onions. No heating is needed.

Pack down onions so that vinegar comes over the onions; add more vinegar if needed. Cover and refrigerate 2–3 days before using. Can be refrigerated 2–3 months; onions will soften.

Because these jars are neither heated nor vacuum-sealed, an airtight closure is not necessary. Any jar and lid will be fine.

Russian Beet Salad

SPECIAL EQUIPMENT: 6-QT. STAINLESS STEEL SAUCEPAN, BOX GRATER OR FOOD PROCESSOR
SERVINGS: 4–6, WHEN SERVED WITH ANY SUMMER SALAD

1 bunch beets

Cool water

1 Tbsp. coarse Dijon mustard

2 Tbsp. plain yogurt

1 Tbsp. sour cream

1 tsp. raw honey

¼ tsp. sea salt

⅛ tsp. black pepper

1 tsp. dill, finely minced

Remove beet tops, and place beets in 6-qt. pot. Cover with cool water about 2″ above beets. Bring to a boil, reduce heat to medium-low, and continue to cook up to 1 hour. Strain beets and immerse in cool water. While in cool water, slip the skins off the beets.

Meanwhile, whisk remaining ingredients together in a large bowl.

Shred the beets with a box grater, or food processor with grating attachment, over the bowl of mixed ingredients.

This can be refrigerated up to one week.

CROP NOTES: *We often utilize larger beets for this salad, and although boiling versus salt roasting (recipe, page 147) loses a bit of the flavor, this recipe is better prepared with skins removed. We find that a boiled beet is easier to skin than a roasted one. The addition of roasted garlic cloves (recipe, page 51) and 1¼ to 1½ c. pickled red onions works wonderfully.*

Braised Beef Short Ribs

2 lb. beef short ribs, 4–6 pieces

½ gal. Basic Meat Brine
(recipe, page 39)

2 Tbsp. canola oil or lard

2 tsp. sea salt, plus more for meat

¼ tsp. black pepper, plus more
for meat

2 qts. beef broth

1 sprig rosemary

4 sprigs sage

2 sprigs thyme

1 bunch early carrots, 4″ or less,
whole

1 bunch early spring red turnips,
halved and up to 3″ stem intact

1 lb. new red potatoes, whole

1 bunch early spring onions, fresh,
halved, and up to 3″ stem intact

1 fennel bulb, cored and julienned

1 lb. asparagus

2 Tbsp. olive oil

Combine ribs and brine in large container; cover and refrigerate overnight. Strain and pat dry when ready to prepare. Heat oil in skillet over medium-high heat, season ribs with salt and pepper, and sear meat until all sides are deep brown.

Preheat oven to 275°.

Place meat in baking dish, add broth and herbs, cover, and bake for 2½ hours.

Remove from oven and uncover. Nestle carrots, turnips, potatoes, onions, and fennel around the ribs. The liquid level should come ¾ up the ribs; add water if needed. Re-cover, and bake an additional 1½ hours. Remove from oven and let rest.

Meanwhile, increase oven temperature to 400°. Toss the asparagus with olive oil, season with 2 tsp. salt and ¼ tsp. black pepper, place on baking sheet, and roast for 10–12 minutes.

Remove ribs from pan and set aside. Ladle ⅓ of the vegetables and broth into blender, or bowl if using an immersion blender. Start slowly and blend to a smooth puree. Pour the puree over a serving platter and place ribs atop the puree. Ladle additional braised vegetables over and around the ribs. Top with the asparagus.

> **CHEF'S NOTE:** This complement of vegetables is decidedly spring. They are equally beautiful simply tossed together with the herbs, salt, and olive oil and roasted. As the seasons change, any number of substitutes will become available through to winter's storage of Cape White turnips, parsnips, russets, and carrots.

Salt Roasted Beets

1 bunch beets, 8–10 golf-ball-sized, greens intact

1 c. kosher salt

1 Tbsp. extra virgin olive oil

Preheat oven to 400°.

Cut beets in half from root to base of stems. Gently pull apart so each beet half has leaves still attached to the stalk.

On a lined baking sheet, pour salt in a line along one side. Place the cut beets on salt line with greens laid out over rest of pan. Drizzle all beet parts with oil. Cover with foil and bake 50–60 minutes. After 50 minutes, remove foil and test doneness with a fork. If the fork slides in and out easily, they are done. Remove from oven.

At this point the greens will be very crisp. They can be crumbled and placed on top of a salad or eaten as chips. The beets can be cut up further as desired to place in a salad.

CHEF'S NOTE: Salt crust roasting pulls out excess moisture and intensifies flavor. If you like things less salty, just cut down on the salt a bit.

CROP NOTES: *Roasting young beets in this manner allows for the flavored skins to remain. Larger, mature beets are usually headed to the pot for a long boil. Greens from the young beets are tender and sweet, great quickly sautéed with extra virgin olive oil and lemon. The leaves also make good chips, and the texture is a great contrast with soft leaves in a salad.*

Colorful Deviled Eggs

SPECIAL EQUIPMENT: BLENDER, 2 ZIPLOCK BAGS, ONE COFFEE FILTER OR CHEESECLOTH, BAKING SHEET
YIELD: 20 DEVILED EGG HALVES

Recipe contributed by Gabrielle Redner: "These eggs were first created for a grand-opening party at Slip Away Farm on Chappaquiddick. They were then featured in a Martha's Vineyard Times *story about a Slow Food Martha's Vineyard event about local eggs, called Coop de Ville. They are a great party snack, and are especially fun to make with friends and kids.*

"This recipe takes two days. Day one is boiling and dyeing the eggs, which should take one hour or less. The eggs must sit in their dye overnight. Day two is making the fillings and filling the eggs. This process takes 1–2 hours. Read recipe through before starting for best results."

INGREDIENTS:

1 dozen eggs

2 tsp. mustard

1 lemon

⅔ c. canola oil

2 medium beets, raw

2 tablespoons and 1 teaspoon of turmeric powder

½ c. packed spinach, nasturtium leaves, or other dark greens

salt

DAY 1: BOIL, PEEL, CUT, AND DYE EGGS.

Boil the eggs: Bring a pot of water to a boil. Place 10 eggs in the boiling water and set a timer for 10 minutes. ☉ Keep the water at a gentle boil. In the meantime, fill a large bowl with ice and cold water. After 10 minutes, immediately place eggs in the ice bath to stop the cooking.

Tip: If you buy your eggs from Morning Glory, they are going to be very fresh, likely not more than one day old. Fresh eggs are harder to peel. Stick a safety pin or a sewing needle into the rounded end of the eggshell before placing eggs in boiling water. This will create an air pocket and make the fresh eggs easier to peel.

Dye for purple eggs: Peel the beets and roughly chop. Place them in a blender with 2 cups of water, and blend until color is rich fuchsia. Strain the solids out by placing a colander over a bowl and lining it with cheesecloth or a coffee filter. Reserve the solid beet puree for the pink filling.

Dye for yellow eggs: Whisk or blend 2 tablespoons of turmeric powder with 2 cups of water.

continued on page 150

Colorful Deviled Eggs *(continued)*

Peel, cut, and dye the eggs: Once cooled, peel eggs under gently running water. Slice them in half vertically. Scoop out the yolks and reserve in a separate container. ☉ Gently rinse away any lingering egg yolk from the whites. ☉ Place 7 boiled egg halves into each dye. ☉ Place remaining 6 egg halves in separate container to leave white. ☉ Cover all three containers and refrigerate overnight.

DAY 2: MAKE THE DEVILED EGG FILLING, FILL THE EGGS, SERVE

For the mayonnaise: Crack two eggs and pour off the whites to save or discard. For the mayonnaise, you will only need the yolks. ☉ Put the yolks into a bowl. ☉ Add 2 tsp. of mustard and the juice of ½ of a lemon, and whisk together. Keep the other ½ lemon on hand. ☉ While whisking vigorously, slowly drizzle the canola oil into the yolk mixture. Use a squeeze bottle or measuring cup with a spout for the oil, and pour in a slow, steady stream. ☉ Keep whisking as you pour, until the oil is fully incorporated and the mayonnaise has thickened. ☉ Taste, and season with salt according to your preference.

For the green filling: Place the nasturtium leaves, spinach, or other greens in a blender. ☉ Add ¼ cup of mayonnaise, ⅓ of the cooked egg yolks, and a pinch of salt. ☉ Blend or process, scraping down the sides when necessary to keep the blade spinning. ☉ Add lemon juice one squeeze at a time if mixture needs thinning. ☉ The mixture should be thick like store-bought mayonnaise, and green. Little flecks of green leaves are fine and pretty. ☉ Using a spatula, move green filling to a plastic, ziplock bag.

For the yellow filling: Rinse out blender. ☉ Add ¼ cup of mayonnaise, ⅓ of the cooked egg yolks, 1 tsp. turmeric powder, and a pinch of salt to the blender. ☉ Blend and wipe down sides as necessary. Add lemon juice to flavor and thin. ☉ The mixture should be thick, smooth, and deep yellow. ☉ Using a spatula, move the yellow filling to another ziplock bag.

For the pink filling: Rinse out blender. ☉ Add remaining mayonnaise and cooked egg yolks, as well as 1 Tbsp. of solid beet puree (reserved from yesterday) and a pinch of salt to the blender. ☉ Blend and push the sides down as necessary. ☉ The mixture will be pink, and looser than the yellow and green fillings. ☉ Using a spatula, move the pink filling into the third ziplock bag.

To fill eggs: Line a cookie sheet with paper towels. ⊙ Strain the purple eggs and place them cut-side down on the cookie sheet, to pour off residual liquid. ⊙ Strain the yellow eggs, giving them a quick rinse to wash off residual turmeric, and place cut-side down on cookie sheet. ⊙ Line white eggs cut-side up on cookie sheet. ⊙ Using a sharp knife, cut off about 1 centimeter from one corner of each ziplock bag. ⊙ Turn the colored eggs cut side up. If liquid remains in center of egg, dry with a paper towel. ⊙ Fill the eggs by squeezing the filling in each bag toward the cut tip, and then squeeze into center of each egg until it fills the hole where the yolk once was. ⊙ Mix and match colors as desired. ⊙ Display and eat!

GLORIOUS BEETS

Like diamonds in the dirt, the earth-stained skin of the beet belies the radiance
of what is beneath. Magnificent fuchsia, golden yellow, or playfully candy-striped,
Morning Glory grows three types of beets. From June through November, you
will find red beets at the stand. Golden and Chioggia beets, more sensitive
to environmental stress, make their presence during the hottest months.

They taste like sweetness and earth, and have a texture all
their own. Boiled, roasted, grilled, or steamed, they are tender
yet firm; they slice like butter but hold their shape.

Generally, the younger the beet, the tastier (and more vibrant) the greens.
The more vibrant the greens, the tastier the beet. But it's not always true, says
Jim Athearn. You can't always judge a beet by its greens. And you can't always
measure its age by its girth. Whether a beet is one inch or three is about
what "opportunities it had," explains Jim, not how long it's been around.

Redding's Beet Hummus

One 15-oz. can chickpeas or ½ c. dried chickpeas, cooked earlier

1 c. kosher salt, optional for roasting beets

2 lb. beets, tops removed

½ tsp. sea salt

1 tsp. ground cumin

1 Tbsp. tahini

½ tsp. cayenne pepper

1 Tbsp. lemon juice

¼ c. extra virgin olive oil

If using dried chickpeas, soak overnight in 4 cups cool water. Strain, cook in fresh water until soft. Immerse in cool water until cool, strain, and dry.

If using canned chickpeas, rinse, strain, and dry.

Preheat oven to 375°.

If roasting beets, pour a line of kosher salt onto parchment-lined baking sheet, place beets on salt, cover with foil and bake 50–60 minutes, until fork tender.

If boiling beets, place beets in pot and cover with cool water. Bring to rolling boil, then lower heat to gently boil beets. When fork tender, immerse in cold water and strain. Remove skins when cool enough to touch, then cool completely.

Coarse cut beets and place in food processor with chickpeas. Pulse until they begin to break up. Add salt, cumin, tahini, cayenne, and lemon juice; pulse to incorporate. Drizzle in olive oil and process until paste is smooth. Additional oil may be required for desired consistency. If roasting beets, they may need more oil.

Redding enjoys serving the hummus with green bell peppers and toasted sourdough.

Gaby's Beet Soup

10 medium red beets, washed not peeled

2 Tbsp. olive oil, plus about ¼ c.

1 head of garlic

2 c. onions, julienned

½ c. white wine, whatever you might drink with dinner

6 c. commercial or homemade vegetable stock

1 Tbsp. fresh thyme

salt and pepper to taste

Preheat the oven to 375°. Clean beets and remove the greens, and sprinkle with olive oil and a pinch of salt. Bake, covered, for 1 hour, or until a fork meets no resistance when piercing the beet. Let cool and peel with a towel.

Simultaneously, bake your garlic. Take the whole head and drizzle it with olive oil and a pinch of salt. Wrap it well in foil, so that the foil is hugging its skin and no air gets in. This should take 30 minutes. To test doneness, unwrap the garlic and squeeze. The cloves should be completely soft.

Sauté julienned onions in 2 Tbsp. of olive oil—in a pot you will use for making the soup—over low heat, until translucent and starting to caramelize, about 15 minutes. Immediately after putting the onions in the pot, season with salt, pepper, and thyme.

Cut the root end off the garlic head, and squeeze the cloves into the pot. Turn up the heat to medium-high, and pour in the white wine. Let it simmer over medium heat until it thickens like a glaze, about 2–3 minutes. Do not let it get dry or burn.

Add the roasted beets, and stir the ingredients in the pot. Add the vegetable stock. Let the soup simmer for 20 minutes. It should not be at a rapid boil.

Transfer the soup to a blender or food processor. Do not fill too high, and cover the air hole only with a towel. Be careful if you are doing this while soup is still hot. Puree, and add the additional olive oil slowly, while pureeing. This may need to be done in two batches depending on the size of your device. Taste, and add salt and pepper if necessary. If the soup is too thick, add water or extra vegetable stock.

Serve immediately, hot, or the next day, chilled.

STRAWBERRIES
The Most Delicious of Crops

The field crew carried in the last strawberries of the season in bright green pint containers on the morning of July 4 last year. Debbie Athearn, co-owner of Morning Glory and the force behind the farm stand, arranged them on the front table. A handwritten sign read, "Our own strawberries, $5.45/pint, the last of the season."

In 2013, between June 5 and July 4, the Morning Glory field crew harvested 4,496 pints of strawberries—a shorter season than most years. The crew carries wooden trays lined neatly with 12 pint containers into the field, where they crouch down low and fill their trays pint by pint, at a speed mostly determined by the density of ripe strawberries on a plant.

At the height of the season, members of the field crew picked strawberries for six hours a day. They inevitably ended up eating some. Well, many.

The nearly 4,500 pints in 2013 is only half the yield of previous years, which put more pressure on finding each ripe berry before it rots. For some reason, many plants did not survive the winter, despite the straw cover that protects their buds-to-be from the cold.

"It changes every year, that's for sure," Simon Athearn says, referring to the financial significance of strawberries to the farm stand. If the yield is low, and the field crew has to painstakingly eke out pockets of the luscious fruit, the cost of labor soars, but the cost of strawberries can only rise so high.

Higher prices do not deter customers. Even some of Morning Glory's dedicated wholesale accounts—chefs and caterers—came to buy strawberries at the stand at regular retail price, since wholesale had such limited quantities. The strawberries are smaller, more tender, and often sweeter than their supermarket counterparts—and, unlike the berries that line grocery store shelves all year round, Morning Glory strawberries are only available for about a month.

On this July 4, the early birds came and whisked away the season's last strawberries in minutes. At 9:20 there were twenty-eight pints left. Twelve minutes later, they were gone. A new sign appeared. "Sadly, our strawberries are all done for the year. 7/4/13."

Of course, a few ripe, deep red fruits still studded plants in the field. They were there to be plucked by any Morning Glory employee who, on his or her own time, wanted to bid June farewell, in one savored bite. Within a few days of the final official harvest, Jim Athearn mows them off with the brush cutter, a necessary part of maintaining the plants for the next season.

"I often get off the tractor, look around, find *one*," Jim pauses as the thought traveled to his taste buds. "Ahh. And then I mow them all off. And that's it, until next June."

Summer Pasta Salad
with tomatoes and strawberries

1 lb. boneless, skinless chicken breasts, trimmed of fat

Water to cover, plus more for pasta

1 c. fresh strawberries or others you may like

1 large red bell pepper, diced

1 medium cucumber, diced

1 c. cherry tomatoes, halved or quartered

1 tbsp. fresh basil

1 tsp. fresh grated lime zest

8 oz. whole-wheat penne or spiral pasta

3 tbsp. extra-virgin olive oil

1 small shallot, finely chopped

½ c. reduced-sodium chicken broth

½ c. crumbled feta cheese

3 tbsp. lime juice

¼ tsp. lite (reduced sodium) salt or Lo-salt

Recipe contributed by Vineyard Nutrition

Place chicken in a skillet and add enough water to cover. Bring to a boil. Cover, reduce heat to low, and simmer gently until cooked through (165°) and no longer pink in the middle, 10–12 minutes.

While chicken is cooking, prepare the strawberries, vegetables, basil, and lime zest and juice (zest lime prior to juicing).

When chicken is done, transfer it to a cutting board to cool.

Bring a large pot of water to a boil. Cook pasta until just tender according to package.

Shred chicken into bite-sized strips. Drain pasta. Add pasta and chicken to a large bowl.

To make the dressing: Heat a small skillet over medium-low heat. Add oil and shallot. Cook, stirring occasionally, until soft and beginning to brown, 2–5 minutes. Add broth, feta, and lime juice and cook, stirring occasionally, until the feta starts to melt, 1–2 minutes.

Pour the dressing over the chicken and pasta. Add berries, bell pepper, cucumber, tomatoes, basil, lime zest, and salt. Toss to combine.

Salt to taste.

Eggy French Toast with Fresh Fruit

2 ½ c. fresh fruit (strawberries, peaches, etc.)

6 eggs

1 ½ c. low-fat milk

1 tbsp. vanilla extract

½ tsp. cinnamon, or as desired

Canola oil cooking spray

8 slices of 100% whole-wheat or whole-grain bread

Recipe contributed by Vineyard Nutrition

To make dipping sauce, put fruit in a blender (or use immersion blender); blend until smooth.

Whisk eggs, milk, vanilla extract and cinnamon together in a shallow 9x13-inch baking dish.

Soak bread slices in the mixture until saturated, then turn each piece over to saturate the other side.

Heat a large skillet on medium heat (or use nonstick griddle) and spray with a small amount of canola oil. When warm, place bread slices in the skillet.

Cook for 2–3 minutes on one side, turn bread over with spatula, and cook for another 2–3 minutes. Make sure they are cooked through before serving.

Serve as strips or shapes with the fruit dipping sauce.

PLANTING AND MAINTAINING STRAWBERRY PLANTS

Each year, one acre of strawberries is planted in May, but the new planting's fruits will not be harvested until June of the following year. The plant is indulged for one full season, when it is weeded, fertilized, and the blossoms pinched, to prepare it for next year's harvest.

The strawberries in the farm stand are harvested from two older acres of strawberry plants, a one-year-old planting and a two-year-old planting. After reaching two years of age, the strawberry plants are plowed under. The weeds in that patch have become too aggressive to continue to maintain. The one-year-old plants are cut back, watered, fertilized, and generally tended to in order to come back plentiful and delicious in their second year.

It takes one year of maintenance before a new plant will produce a substantial yield. So the same season a new acre is planted, a one-year-old acre of plants and a two-year-old acre of plants are harvested.

Cottage Cheese Pancakes with Fresh Fruit

SPECIAL EQUIPMENT: BLENDER, IMMERSION BLENDER, OR FOOD PROCESSOR, LARGE SKILLET OR GRIDDLE / SERVINGS: 4

Fruit, such as strawberries or peaches, diced

1 c. low-fat cottage cheese

4 eggs

¼ c. skim milk

2 tbsp. canola oil

½ tsp. vanilla extract (optional)

½ c. whole-wheat flour

¼ c. cinnamon

Canola oil cooking spray

Recipe contributed by Vineyard Nutrition

To make dipping sauce, put fruit in a blender (or use immersion blender) and blend until smooth. Set aside.

Puree cottage cheese in food processor (or use immersion blender); add eggs, milk, oil, and vanilla extract and mix. Add flour and cinnamon; mix until smooth.

Heat a large skillet or griddle over medium heat; spray with canola oil.

Pour ¼ cup mixture per pancake on skillet or griddle. Cook for 2–3 minutes. Turn over with spatula and cook for 2–3 minutes, making sure they are cooked through before serving.

Serve with fruit dipping sauce.

Spring Kale Salad

1 bunch kale, 8–10 leaves, stems removed

1 c. strawberries, hulled, halved or quartered

½ c. Pickled Hakurei Turnips (recipe, page 136)

1 bunch globe radishes, halved, 2″ stem remaining

8 oz. fresh feta, crumbled (we use Mermaid Farm's)

½ tsp. sea salt

¼ tsp. cracked black pepper

1 tsp. tarragon, finely minced

Loose leaves of kale—lacinato, curly-leaf, and red Russian—tower above the other veggies in edible bouquets. Massaged with vinaigrette and eaten raw, cooked and served as a side, coated in creamy dressing, again the uses are many.

Hand-tear kale into bite-sized pieces. Arrange salad in layers as desired, or toss. Sprinkle with salt and pepper. Use a light dressing to liven up the dish.

Summer Water

1 cucumber, quartered and sliced

1 lemon, sliced

5 sprigs mint

1 sprig cilantro

Strawberry or rhubarb stalk

Recipe contributed by Joan Chaput of West Tisbury

Fill pitcher with 6 cups cold water.

Add cucumber, lemon, mint, and cilantro.

Let stand at least 8 hours, or up to 1 day.

Serve over ice and garnish with a strawberry or rhubarb.

Yogurt and Granola Parfaits

2 c. plain, low-fat regular or Greek yogurt

1 c. low-sugar granola

2 c. strawberries

2 tsp. real maple syrup, optional

Recipe from Vineyard Nutrition

Spoon ¼ cup yogurt into each glass, then add 2 Tbsp. granola, then add ¼ cup berries. Repeat once for each glass.

If using, drizzle ½ tsp. maple syrup on top of each parfait.

Other toppings to try: coconut flakes, ground or slivered nuts, ground flax or chia seeds, dried fruit, or other kinds of fresh fruit.

Strawberry Shortcake

SPECIAL EQUIPMENT: BAKING SHEET. MIXER TO WHIP CREAM / MAKES: 12 BISCUITS

SHORTCAKE BISCUITS

2 c. all-purpose flour, plus more for floured surface

1 tsp. cream of tartar

½ tsp. baking soda

½ tsp. sea salt

3 Tbsp. granulated sugar

5 Tbsp. unsalted butter, cold, cut into ½–2″ pieces

1 c. milk, cold

FILLING

1 pint strawberries, hulled and halved

1 Tbsp. evaporated cane juice (or sugar)

½ tsp. lemon juice

¼ tsp. sea salt

8–10 leaves basil, cut into fine ribbons

Fresh cream—sour cream, crème fraiche, or marscapone

Whipping cream

Preheat oven to 400°.

In a medium mixing bowl, whisk together flour, cream of tartar, baking soda, salt, and sugar.

Toss cold butter into flour mixture, then cut butter into mixture using pastry cutter, forks, or fingers, looking for a shaggy consistency with flat lumps of butter.

Stir in cold milk just until combined, forming a craggy dough.

Turn out onto lightly floured surface and press to ¾″ height. Cut desired shape and arrange on parchment-lined baking sheet.

Bake 12–15 minutes, turning sheet halfway through for an even bake. Cook until tops are golden brown.

Cool at last 10–15 minutes before using for shortcakes.

(Optional: brush with egg wash and sprinkle with turbinado sugar just before baking.)

For Filling: Combine strawberries, cane juice or sugar, lemon juice, sea salt and basil in a bowl and let sit for one hour.

Whip cream.

Slice the biscuits in half and spread 1 Tbsp. of the fresh cream on bottom biscuit. Spoon on strawberries and whipped cream. Top with other half of the biscuit.

SUMMER SQUASH
Breakfast, Lunch, and Dinner

Summer squash is that everyday crop that, like potatoes but less caloric and starchy, can insert itself effortlessly into breakfast (summer hash with potatoes and herbs), lunch (grilled and layered onto a crusty baguette with roasted red peppers, caramelized onions, and maybe some fresh mozzarella), and dinner (marinated in rounds, grilled as a kebab, and served with grilled fish or meat).

It can be a treat, baked into zucchini bread, or a component of a refreshing summer juice, often a part of the Green Monster at the Morning Glory juice bar.

Zucchini, pattypan, crookneck, and yellow squash are all part of the same squash family, *cucurbita pepo,* characterized by prickly leaves and stems that, unfortunately, cause a red and scratchy rash to those who harvest it—making it one of the field crew's more difficult and heaviest crops to harvest.

If summer squash are left on the plant long enough, they develop a deeper color, a hardened rind, and large seeds. They lose their culinary appeal, becoming bitter or watery on the inside. Even just a couple of extra days in the field and the squash will become too big for sale. Luckily, on a farm with a busy kitchen and bakery, overgrown but still tasty squash will be well-used in zucchini bread.

The most robust of the summer squash is surely the crookneck. Warty, bent at the neck, and with seeds aplenty, the crookneck squash looks like a yellow squash gone wrong. But for many, this is their farm stand favorite, an heirloom variety of the straighter-necked yellow squash. The crookneck squash has been grown for many years, was a subject of writings by Thomas Jefferson, and is native to New Jersey.

Most importantly is the fact (or widespread opinion) that its flavor is delicious: it is buttery and rich. Its texture is meaty. Its skin is soft enough to eat but still has substance. Its seeds, plentiful and tender, spill out beautifully, like treasure from a chest, after the squash is cooked and cut open.

Crookneck Squash Potage

1½–2 lb. young crookneck squash, 6 medium

2 Tbsp. extra virgin olive oil, divided

1 tsp. sea salt, divided

2 Tbsp. butter

1½–2 c. onion, diced

½ c. leek, white only, cut lengthwise, then across

¾ c. celery, 2 ribs, diced

1 Tbsp. thyme, minced

2 Tbsp. raw, unfiltered apple cider vinegar

1 tsp. lemon zest

½ tsp. nutmeg

2 qts. commercial or homemade vegetable stock

2 lb. potatoes, skins on, washed, coarsely chopped

½ tsp. black pepper

Cheese for garnish (we suggest Shy Brothers Cloumage, a soft, tangy cheese like crème fraiche)

Preheat oven to 375°.

Wash and cut stem from squash; slice in half lengthwise. Coat with ½ tsp. olive oil and sprinkle with ½ tsp. salt. Place cut side down on lined baking sheet; bake 30 minutes or until skin blisters and squash is soft.

Meanwhile, in 6-qt. saucepan melt butter and remaining oil over medium, medium-high heat. Add onions, remaining salt, leek, celery, and thyme, sauté 7–8 minutes until softened. Add vinegar, lemon zest, and nutmeg, stir and cook 2 minutes. Add stock and potatoes, boil, reduce heat to medium-low, and simmer 45–60 minutes, until potatoes are tender.

Add squash; puree using blender or immersion blender until smooth. Add pepper, garnish with cheese.

CHEF'S NOTE: Young squash do not need to be seeded, as the skins and seeds will be tender. A more mature or larger squash will need to be seeded. Crookneck, when roasted, will provide a flavor unmatched by any of our other summer squash varieties.

Balsamic Roasted Vegetables

FOR DRESSING

2 Tbsp. balsamic vinegar

1 tsp. Dijon mustard

⅓ c. extra virgin olive oil

3 garlic cloves, pressed

2 tsp. finely chopped fresh thyme

1 tsp. basil

Kosher salt and pepper to taste

2 large red onions, halved and thinly sliced

1 yellow bell pepper, cut into ½-inch-wide strips

1 red pepper, cut into ½-inch-wide strips

1 orange bell pepper, cut into ½-inch-wide strips

1 1-lb. eggplant, quartered lengthwise and cut crosswise into ½-inch slices

2 medium yellow squash , cut into ⅓-inch rounds

2 medium zucchini, cut into ⅓-inch rounds

Recipe contributed by Polly Brown of Vineyard Haven

Preheat oven to 450°.

Whisk vinegar and mustard in medium bowl. Gradually whisk in oil. Stir in garlic, thyme, and basil.

Season to taste with salt and pepper. (Dressing can be made a day ahead.)

Place vegetables in a large bowl; sprinkle with salt and pepper. Add dressing and toss to coat.

Divide between baking sheets, over parchment paper or aluminum foil. Roast until the vegetables are tender and slightly brown around the edges, about 35 minutes.

Serve warm or cold.

TIPS ON GLUTEN-FREE BAKING

✳ Make sure batter isn't cold when it goes in the oven. Be sure all ingredients come up to room temperature before mixing.

✳ If batter is cooler than room temperature, allow it to rest next to the preheating oven to come up to room temperature (do this with cakes as well).

✳ When making gluten-free zucchini bread, pressing out the moisture prevents the loaf from becoming gummy in the center.

✳ If tea breads and cakes are coming out gummy, or falling after baking, check the oven's temperature. Some ovens never quite reach the proper temperature. This can be adjusted by baking items longer or increasing the temperature. If the oven temperature is not the issue, start adding a tablespoon or two less liquid to batters. Humidity may cause flours to absorb moisture in the environment; too much moisture can make for a gummy product.

Gluten-Free Zucchini Bread

SPECIAL EQUIPMENT: STAND MIXER OR HAND MIXER, LOAF PAN OR MUFFIN TIN / YIELD: 1 LOAF OR 8 MUFFINS

Non-stick spray for pan

1 c. fresh zucchini, grated

2 oz. sorghum flour

8 oz. gluten-free all-purpose flour

1.5 oz. tapioca starch or flour

1 Tbsp. baking powder

1 tsp. baking soda

1¾ tsp. xanthan gum

1 tsp. sea salt

1 tsp. cinnamon

12 oz. brown sugar

¼ c. olive oil

¼ c. coconut oil

1 tsp. fresh lemon juice

2 eggs

¾ c. coconut milk

⅓ c. chopped walnuts or pecans (optional)

Preheat oven to 375°.

Spray loaf pan with pan spray, or line muffin tin.

Press the grated zucchini with a paper towel to remove as much moisture as possible. After pressing, fluff with fork.

In a large mixing bowl, whisk together dry ingredients; add brown sugar.

Add oils, lemon juice, eggs, and coconut milk. Beat to combine and continue to beat on medium high until the batter is smooth, 2 minutes.

Stir in zucchini and nuts (if using) by hand. Scoop batter into prepared loaf pan and level the top.

Bake in the center of oven. Rotate the pan after 45 minutes. Continue baking until top is golden brown and firm, yet gives a bit when lightly touched. It should feel slightly springy. This may take an additional 25–30 minutes.

CHEF'S NOTE: This lovely gluten-free zucchini bread can be prepared with or without eggs, since the recipe contains sufficient leavening and moisture. And it's dairy-free. Its delicate flavor and texture come from a secret ingredient: coconut milk.

CROP NOTES: *Zucchini has a much higher water content picked fresh at the beginning through the middle of the season. Store-bought or late-season zucchini will have little excess moisture when pressing to dry.*

Chicken and Zucchini

8 oz. whole-wheat egg noodles

14 oz. reduced-sodium chicken broth

1 lb. boneless, skinless chicken breasts, diced into 1″ cubes

6 c. zucchini

1½ c. skim milk

½ c. low-fat mayonnaise

3 Tbsp. whole-wheat flour

1½ tsp. dry mustard

½ tsp. garlic powder

¼ tsp. salt

¼ tsp. ground black pepper

1½ c. reduced-fat Cheddar or Colby-Jack cheese, shredded

Recipe contributed by Vineyard Nutrition

Place noodles in skillet. Add broth, chicken, and zucchini.

Whisk milk, mayonnaise, flour, dry mustard, garlic powder, salt, and pepper in a medium bowl. Pour over zucchini.

Bring to a simmer over medium-high heat. Reduce heat to medium, cover, and simmer until noodles and chicken are cooked, 15–18 minutes, stirring occasionally.

Meanwhile, position oven rack in upper third of oven. Preheat broiler.

When dish is done cooking on the stove, sprinkle cheese on top and transfer to oven. Broil until lightly browned, 3 minutes.

Zucchini Ribbons with Lime, Garlic, and Mint

SPECIAL EQUIPMENT: JULIENNE PEELER, LARGE NONSTICK SKILLET / SERVINGS: 4 AS A SIDE DISH

1 lb. young zucchini or yellow squash, ends trimmed, washed and dried

1 ½ Tbsp. unsalted butter

1 large clove garlic, smashed

½ tsp. kosher salt, more to taste

2 tsp. fresh lime juice

2 Tbsp. toasted pine nuts or sliced almonds, finely chopped

1 Tbsp. fresh cilantro, mint, or a combination, chopped

Recipe contributed by Susie Middleton, cookbook author and West Tisbury farmer

Working over a large mixing bowl, peel the squash lengthwise with a julienne peeler into thin strips. Work all the way around the squash until the thick seed core. Discard the core. Break the strips up with your hands, as they tend to clump together.

In a large nonstick skillet, heat the butter over medium-high heat. When the butter has melted, add the smashed garlic clove and cook, occasionally flattening the clove with a spatula, just until the butter and garlic start to turn a light brown. Remove the garlic. Add the squash strips and the salt. Cook, tossing with tongs, until the squash becomes pliable, 1 minute.

Remove the pan from heat and add the lime juice and most of the chopped nuts and herbs; toss well. Taste and season with salt if desired. Serve garnished with remaining nuts and herbs.

> **NOTE FROM SUSIE:** "This is a recipe I developed to use a cool little hand-tool called a julienne peeler. It doesn't cost much and makes the most beautiful fine ribbons of summer squash. Peel lengthwise until you get to the seedy core (feed that to the chickens!). The ribbons need only a quick turn in the sauté pan to be perfectly cooked."

HERBS FOR COOKING—AND SMELLING

Rosemary Confalone is the full-time manager of the herb garden at Morning Glory. She estimates that there are almost sixty herbs and herb varietals growing there, such as the four varieties of edible and beautiful nasturtium, three of thyme, and two of sage.

A tour of the garden makes it clear that within the vast world of herbs, just a sparse selection have risen to the heights of popularity. But luckily, Morning Glory hasn't excluded those that are less easily understood.

Perceived flavor is not just about taste but also aroma. Herbs are incredibly aromatic. In addition an herb, munched raw, may taste bitter or sweet. But in cooking, it will release its essential oils and add a depth of flavor to the foods it accompanies.

Summer Vegetable Tian

SPECIAL EQUIPMENT: 6-QT. SAUCEPAN, 9X13" PAN / SERVINGS: 8

2 qts. water

2 tsp. sea salt, divided, plus one pinch for boiling water

1 tsp. lemon juice

3 zucchini, medium, sliced in ¼" rounds

3 summer squash, medium, sliced in ¼" rounds

1 eggplant, medium, cut lengthwise, sliced in ¼" half moons

2 red bell peppers, stemmed, seeds and membrane removed, sliced in 4 panels

2 yellow bell peppers, stemmed, seeds and membrane removed, sliced in 4 panels

2 Tbsp. extra virgin olive oil

1 tsp. fennel seed

10 oz. jar red pepper sauce or 10 oz. Deb's Garden Special (recipe, page 191)

4 plum tomatoes, sliced lengthwise, cut into 4–5 slices per tomato

1 Tbsp. finely minced herbs, such as summer savory, oregano, marjoram, rosemary

½ c. fresh bread crumbs

Preheat oven to 375°.

In 6-qt. saucepan, boil water, adding a pinch of salt and lemon juice. Add zucchini and summer squash, blanch 30 seconds, remove with slotted spoon, and place in strainer. Place strainer into a cold water bath for 3 minutes. Drain and set aside.

Place eggplant and peppers in large bowl; toss with olive oil. Spread onto lined baking sheet. Sprinkle with 1 tsp. salt and fennel seed. Bake 18–20 minutes, or until vegetables give to the touch. The pepper skins will begin to blister, and the eggplant changes color to a soft, glistening tan.

Meanwhile, line a 9x13" pan with red pepper sauce. If using Deb's Garden Special, puree or blend until smooth. Tomato sauce may be used as well.

Arrange vegetables over sauce in baking pan. Place in rows of overlapping pieces, creating lines across alternating zucchini, eggplant, red pepper, summer squash, tomato, yellow pepper. Repeat until pan is full. Sprinkle with herbs, remaining salt, and bread crumbs. Bake 30–35 minutes.

TOMATOES
A Really Local Crop

Morning Glory tomatoes are, quite literally, a homegrown crop. In the deep of winter, Debbie Athearn shifts furniture in her dining room to make room for tomatoes. She plants seeds in the place where she and Jim eat and host. "We still have a dining room," she says cheerfully. "It's just a little more compact."

Three weeks later, Debbie replants them to give each plant more space and the chance to build stronger roots. No longer able to fit in the dining room, Debbie moves them into the farm stand's walk-in refrigerator, now heated and fitted with grow lights, to trick the tomatoes into thinking it's summertime. Once the plants are six to eight inches tall, they are moved into the greenhouse where they benefit from the warmth of a wood stove, radiant heating (electric and wind-powered), and the insulation of the double-layered, plastic walls.

Even with additional heat, it's slow growing for these tomatoes, when the weather outside is cold and sunlight is sparse. Yet by early June, the tomatoes are ripe and ready to eat. And, almost always, they are the first fresh tomatoes available on Martha's Vineyard.

Proper care early in the tomato's life prepares the plant to handle stress later. Other factors make it delicious.

Variety and ripeness make the difference between a mealy, bland, red orb and a juicy, sweet, and tangy tomato. Irrigation strategy has an impact on flavor as well: too much watering at critical points of growth can make the tomatoes watery and bland, or conversely, rich with flavor.

There were twenty-nine varieties of tomatoes growing at Morning Glory. To decide which will make it to the next season, the Athearns; Lydia Hall, nicknamed the Tomato Queen; and Chef Robert compare their tomato notes and experiences. They determine which varieties are worth growing again, growing in higher quantity, or leaving behind. There are a slew of criteria that determine a plant's success, including disease resistance, productivity, susceptibility to pests, and size. But flavor is a weighty factor in the decision making process.

"Mom and Dad harp on the importance of flavor all the time," says Simon Athearn. "If the plants struggle to grow, but the tomatoes taste good, we'll still grow it."

Disease resistance is an important factor in selecting all varieties of tomatoes. But it is especially important for those planted in the greenhouse, a structure that is costly to build and run. "There are greenhouse varieties with better disease resistance [than what we choose]," says Simon, "but they just don't taste as good." But then there are also tomatoes that taste great yet simply don't survive.

"Pampered little things," says Debbie, gently placing a Striped German, yellow and pink heirloom, into its place on the front table. It is now September, and the tomato harvest is still going strong. "Everyone likes heirlooms, but they're the most difficult to grow. They crack. They don't produce as much. But they definitely do taste good."

Couscous with Roasted Cherry Tomatoes

SPECIAL EQUIPMENT: 4-QT. POT, LARGE BAKING PAN / SERVINGS: 2–4

1 ½ c. water

1 Tbsp. plus 1 tsp. extra virgin olive oil

1 c. whole-wheat couscous

½ tsp. sea salt, divided

1 bunch scallions, white only, sliced lengthwise, chopped

1 pt. cherry or grape tomatoes, halved or quartered depending on size

¼ tsp. fennel seed

⅛ tsp. cayenne pepper

1 c. chopped spinach

¼ tsp. lemon zest

1 Tbsp. lemon juice

1 Tbsp. flat leaf parsley, finely chopped

1 tsp. mint, finely chopped

4 oz. feta

Preheat oven to 375°.

Boil water in 4-qt. pot; add 1 tsp. oil and ¼ tsp. salt. Add couscous; cover and remove from heat. Let stand 15 minutes.

Meanwhile, toss scallions and tomatoes with remaining oil and salt, fennel seed, and cayenne. Lay on lined baking sheet. Bake 15–18 minutes, until tomatoes caramelize.

Mix spinach, lemon zest, lemon juice, parsley, and mint in bowl. Fluff couscous, add to spinach mixture. Add tomatoes and scallions with the juices and spices from pan. Lightly mix in feta.

Roasted Tomato Vinaigrette

5 roma or plum tomatoes

½ tsp. sea salt

3 oz. raw, unfiltered apple cider vinegar

½ c. basil leaves, lightly packed

1 tsp. raw honey

⅛ tsp. black pepper

1 c. extra virgin olive oil

Preheat oven to 400°.

Cut tomatoes in half lengthwise; place cut side up on lined roasting pan. Sprinkle with salt to help accelerate drying. Roast 45 minutes until flattened and dry and edges are fully caramelized and dark brown. Alternatively, tomatoes can be slowly roasted at 300°; this will take longer, but provide a richer, sweeter flavor.

Place roasted tomatoes, vinegar, basil, honey, and pepper in food processor. Process until smooth, stopping to scrape sides. When smooth, start processor and drizzle in olive oil, blending until completely combined.

Refrigerate up to 3 weeks.

Serenaded Tomatoes

2 pts. assorted varieties of cherry and grape tomatoes, halved or quartered depending on size

¼ tsp. sea salt

½ c. extra virgin olive oil

2 Tbsp. raw, unfiltered apple cider vinegar

1 tsp. raw honey

1 tsp. Dijon mustard

6 medium heirloom tomatoes

Debbie used this colorful, playful dish to entice her children to enjoy tomatoes. It worked. But they couldn't pronounce "marinated" and called them serenaded tomatoes. The colors in this dish, and the sweetness of the ripe cherry tomatoes, would woo just about anyone as much as any serenade could ever do!

Sprinkle the cherry tomatoes with salt.

Whisk together the oil, vinegar, honey, and mustard. Pour over the cherry tomatoes, stir, and let sit at room temperature for 1 hour to serenade—oops! Marinate.

Meanwhile, hollow out heirloom tomatoes by slicing a quarter-sized round off the top, and using a paring knife, melon baller, or grapefruit spoon to cut and scoop away the seeds and core.

After the cherry and grape tomatoes have marinated and just before serving, fill the heirloom tomatoes all the way up with the cherry and grape tomatoes.

> **CHEF'S NOTE:** The apple cider vinegar and honey accentuate the flavors already inherent in tomatoes: sweetness and tang. Ripe tomatoes are usually very sweet, so if you prefer to leave out the honey in the adult version, it will still taste great. Apple cider vinegar is used here in part because it is derived from a delicious and local New England product: apples.

For a more "adult" version (but also quite beautiful) . . .

6 heirloom tomatoes

¼ tsp. sea salt

½ c. extra virgin olive oil

2 Tbsp. raw, unfiltered apple cider vinegar

1 tsp. Dijon mustard

1 tsp. raw honey, optional

Torn or chopped fresh parsley and dill, or other fresh herbs

Cut a thin round off the top of the tomato to remove any brown part on the skin. Continue to slice the tomato in ¼″ rounds, and repeat with all the heirloom tomatoes.

Lay the tomatoes in a baking dish and sprinkle evenly with sea salt.

Whisk together the oil, vinegar, mustard, and honey, if using. Pour over the tomatoes, and let sit at room temperature to marinate for 1 hour.

To serve, lay the tomatoes out, layering each tomato to partially cover the next one; sprinkle with torn herbs.

Kerry Hanney's Tomato Pie

SPECIAL EQUIPMENT: STAND MIXER OR FOOD PROCESSOR, PIE TIN / SERVINGS: 4–6

1 pie crust (recipe, page 184)

1¾ lb. ripe tomatoes, cut into
   ¼″ slices, or quartered

2 c. extra-sharp cheddar cheese,
   grated

¼ c. pecorino Romano, grated, or
   regional hard sheep's milk cheese

2 tsp. sea salt

½ tsp. pepper

2 Tbsp. basil, chopped

1 Tbsp. dill, chopped

1 scallion, thinly sliced

2 Tbsp. cornmeal

Preheat oven to 350°.

Roll out pastry shell between two pieces of parchment paper to 12 inches in diameter. Remove top layer of parchment, lift shell, invert onto pie tin, and trim edges to overhang up to ½ inch.

Cover pastry shell with parchment paper, and weigh down with beans, rice, or pie weights. Bake 20 minutes.

Meanwhile, lay sliced tomatoes on two layers of paper towels to remove some of the moisture.

Combine cheeses, salt, pepper, herbs, and scallion.

After shell has baked, sprinkle cornmeal over the bottom. Spread ½ cup cheese mixture over cornmeal. Make one layer tomatoes; they can overlap. Spread 1 cup cheese mixture over tomatoes. Layer remaining tomatoes and top with remaining cheese mixture.

Bake 20–25 minutes, until bubbling and browning on top.

CROP NOTES: *The cornmeal and cheese will help bind the filling, so choose ripe, moist tomatoes. Early-season, hot-house, or under-ripe fruit will not provide the flavor or moisture required here. Although the baking will lessen the vibrancy of the assorted heirloom's colors, the variety not only provides differing hues but also a more complex flavor.*

Pie Crust

1 c. pastry flour

1 c. high-protein organic bread flour, or 1 c. all-purpose flour

½ tsp. sea salt

4 oz. unsalted butter, cold

4 oz. shortening (whipped palm oil), butter or lard, cold (Note: Morning Glory uses all butter)

¼ c. ice water, to use as needed

Combine flours and salt.

Cut butter and shortening into small cubes. (Morning Glory uses all butter for its pie crusts. It makes the flakiest crusts. Home chefs, however, may prefer to use 50 percent butter and 50 percent other fat.)

In stand mixer fitted with paddle attachment, or food processor, combine half the dry ingredients with the butter and shortening. Mix until it forms cohesive dough. Small chunks of visible butter and shortening are fine.

Add the rest of the dry ingredients and mix briefly until the mixture looks like breadcrumbs or wet crumbly sand. Do not overmix.

Add ice water 1 Tbsp. at a time and mix until dough *just* comes together. Divide into two equal portions, bake a ball, and roll into a disk. Wrap in plastic, chill in refrigerator at least 30 minutes.

Tomato, Bacon, and Onion Jam

Always check safe canning methods at the National Center for Home Food Preservation, www.nchfp.uga.edu

½ lb. bacon, cut into ¼″ strips (we use our end cuts)

1 bay leaf

½ tsp. mustard seed

¼ tsp. red chili flakes

4 medium onions, cut in half and finely julienned

1 tsp. sea salt

2 Tbsp. raw, unfiltered apple cider vinegar

12 roma or plum tomatoes, coarsely chopped into 8 pieces

2 Tbsp. maple syrup

Render bacon in heavy-bottom skillet over medium-low heat. Remove from pan with slotted spoon before fully crisp, but beginning to brown. Leave fat drippings in pan. Add bay leaf, mustard seed, chili flakes, onions, and salt. Cook 10–12 minutes over medium-low heat until onions are soft. Add vinegar and stir to incorporate.

Mix in tomatoes and bacon. Continue cooking over medium-low heat 1 hour, or bake at 350°. The longer it cooks, the smoother the texture of the jam. Fold in maple syrup.

Spoon jam into sterilized canning jars. Press down the solids to let the air and fat push upward. The fat will cool and create a natural seal at the top. Refrigerate. As long as fat layer is on top, it should be good for an extended period of time. See the National Center for Home Food Preservation, mchfp.uga.edu, for safe canning tips.

Warm and serve over a grilled steak or fish.

Warm Eggplant and Tomato Salad

SPECIAL EQUIPMENT: HEAVY-BOTTOM SKILLET / SERVINGS: 6–8

1 medium-sized Italian eggplant, medium dice

2 Tbsp. plus ¼ tsp. sea salt, divided

¼ c. olive oil

1 medium yellow onion, medium dice

1 sprig rosemary

½ tsp. chili pepper flakes or ¼–½ fresh, hot chili pepper, depending on desired heat (cayenne, serrano, jalapeno), minced

1 tsp. fennel seeds

6 tomatoes, heirloom or field, medium dice

This warm salad is so versatile. It can be a bruschetta topping. It can be served hot or cold. It can be a layer in fish tacos, which was the meal that inspired the dish. It is more than a sauce, and when it accompanies meat, poultry, or fish, it can be a stew of sorts, beneath the protein, or a colorful way to top off the dish. It can also be mixed with pasta or beans. Serve with Salt-Crusted Pork Chops (recipe, page 43).

Lay the diced eggplant on a dish towel or two layers of paper towel, and sprinkle evenly with 2 Tbsp. sea salt. Cover with another dish towel or two layers paper towel and let sit 1 hour. Occasionally pat the eggplant with the towels to remove the moisture.

Heat oil in skillet over medium heat. Add onions, rosemary, remaining salt, and dried chili flakes, if using. Sauté until onions are translucent, 5 minutes. Add eggplant, fennel seed, and chili pepper, if using. Stirring occasionally, sauté until eggplant is soft and has turned from white to medium brown.

Add tomatoes to skillet. Turn heat up to medium-high, cook 15 minutes, stirring occasionally.

CROP NOTES: *Salting an eggplant ahead of time helps remove some of the bitterness that comes in big, ripe eggplants, especially the "classic" variety, which is so flavorful. It also helps to remove some of the water in the eggplant, so it will become more compact and absorb less oil. This way, the eggplant will cook fully, but retain its form and not become overly greasy. Many Asian and white varieties lack the same degree of bitterness and, for purposes of flavor, may not need salting.*

Stewed Tomatoes

1 medium yellow onion, julienned

Sea salt

8 ripe tomatoes, coarsely diced

½ c. olive oil, divided

3 bell peppers, julienned

Pepper

1 sprig fresh rosemary

2 1-inch slices fresh-baked bread, plus rest of loaf for serving

Preheat oven to 400°.

Lay onions in bottom of a casserole dish; sprinkle with a pinch of salt. Layer half the tomatoes on top of onions. Pour over ¼ cup olive oil. Top with all the peppers.

Top peppers with remaining tomatoes, and pour over remaining oil. Sprinkle with salt and pepper. Push sprig of rosemary into the middle of the dish. Cover with foil; bake 25 minutes.

Meanwhile, put bread slices in food processor, and pulse to make medium-small breadcrumbs.

Remove tomatoes from oven, uncover, stir in breadcrumbs. Return to oven uncovered. Bake 5–7 minutes.

Serve over toasted slices of bread cut from remaining loaf. This dish can also be an accompaniment to meat or fish, mixed with cannelloni beans and used as a side dish. It is also delicious cold the next day.

CROP NOTES: *This dish is an updated version of Debbie Athearn's traditional family recipe. Use any tomatoes that are too ripe to slice for raw eating. A combination of red and yellow peppers makes for a more colorful dish, but purple peppers will bleed their color, better reserved for raw uses. Morning Glory's country herb loaf is a great bread for this dish, enhancing it with the fresh herbs baked into the crusty loaf.*

Deb's Garden Special with Fresh Cod

SPECIAL EQUIPMENT: 2-GAL. STAINLESS STEEL STOCK POT / YIELD: 11 PINTS. WITH COD: 4 SERVINGS

4 c. onions, diced

6 sweet peppers, green or red,
seeds removed, diced

4 c. water or tomato juice

4 qt. tomatoes

4 c. celery, diced

3 Tbsp. sea salt

FOR FISH

Olive oil

4 good-sized cod fillets

Fresh lemon juice

Sea salt

Black pepper

Smoked paprika

Lemon zest

1 Tbsp. parsley, chopped

In 2-gal. stainless steel stock pot over medium heat, cook onions and peppers in water or tomato juice. Add tomatoes, celery, and salt. Boil 5 minutes and distribute into jars.

Process in hot water bath as per standard canning instructions. We recommend guidelines posted by the National Center for Home Food Preservation: nchfp.uga.edu.

Note on Fish: For entertaining, use the fatter or loin end of the fillet. The narrower, or tail ends can be trimmed and saved for chowder or cod cakes. If using the whole fillet, still cut in half and take the tail end and fold in half over itself, doubling the height. Cooking times should then be equalized on all pieces. A serving size is one fillet per person.

Warm a cast-iron skillet or roasting pan. Drizzle olive oil into pan. Place fish in pan. Drizzle fish with lemon juice. Season the fish with salt, pepper, and paprika. Pour Deb's Garden Special equally over the fillets. Sprinkle the top of the covered fish with the lemon zest. Place the pan in a preheated 400° oven and bake for 15 minutes. Remove from oven. Sprinkle parsley over top and let sit to finish cooking for 5 minutes.

> **CHEF'S NOTE:** This can be a bruschetta topping. It can be served hot or cold. It can be a layer in fish tacos, which was the meal that inspired the dish. It is more than a sauce, and when it accompanies meat, poultry, or fish, it can be a stew of sorts, beneath the protein, or a colorful way to top off the dish. It can also be mixed with pasta or beans.

GLEANERS: LEFTOVERS BECOME THE MAIN DISH

Farming is a guessing game. Farmers grow for a changing market and generally plant more than they need to make sure of a constant supply. Often, that means the food left in fields is over-ripe or not worth the labor to pick.

For years, Jim Athearn, like other farmers on the Island, routinely plowed under thousands of pounds of edible crops. The organic matter fed the soil and nourished the fields.

But Jim had always known those crops could help meet a different need. He knew that the surplus could help to feed an island.

Now, because of the Martha's Vineyard gleaners, it does.

Morning Glory and other farms on the Vineyard donate thousands of pounds of produce each growing season to feed the elderly, schoolchildren, adults with mental illness, and many others who are in need of meals and groceries. The number grew from a few thousand pounds in the early years of organized gleaning to over twenty-three thousand pounds in 2011, '12, and '13. Twenty different organizations participate in the distribution of food, from the Dukes County Jail, to Martha's Vineyard schools, to the Island Food Pantry.

As the largest farm on the Vineyard, Morning Glory provides between eighteen and twenty thousand pounds of crops—picked and sorted by a group of volunteers who are invited into the fields each time the farmer has finished.

"We really rely on this small, core group of gleaners, generally five or six women who just come almost every week and make it happen. They're really dedicated," says Jamie O'Gorman, the coordinator

of the gleaning group on Martha's Vineyard. She, too, is very dedicated, coordinating with farmers, volunteers, and local distribution organizations alike to get the surplus harvest into the hands that can truly benefit from it.

Today the gleaning program is a project of Island Grown Initiative (IGI), a local nonprofit organization. But gleaning actually started on the Vineyard with a group of women farmers who formed an organization called the Sowing Circle. One of their goals was to encourage gleaning, and to connect gleaners with organizations that could get the food to the right people.

"The advantage of the gleaning program is it reaches people who we don't know, but who we know are out there," says Rebecca Gilbert of Native Earth Teaching Farm, previously a member of the Sowing Circle and the coordinator of their gleaning initiative. "It's a culture-changing project."

Gleaning brings people who otherwise wouldn't farm into the fields, and it brings fresh, local produce to people and institutions that otherwise wouldn't have access to it. Gleaning is progressive, and it is ancient.

"When you reap the harvest of your land, you shall not wholly reap the corners of your field when you reap, nor shall you gather any gleaning from your harvest. You shall leave them for the poor and for the stranger."—Leviticus 23:22.

"When I first started finding out about gleaning, I didn't even know what the word was, but then somebody said it was biblical so I looked it up in the Bible and sure enough there it was," says Marilyn Jackson Adams, a regular volunteer who enjoys learning about farming through her gleans and through her niece, who is part of the Morning Glory field crew.

"My passion is feeding people. I've never done it from the ground up, so to speak, so this is a whole different part of that," says Marilyn.

The bridge between an ancient concept and an effective, modern program is cooperation. Farmers and volunteers must work together and trust one another: farmers expect volunteers to stay in designated fields, to harvest and then to drop off the food to recipient organizations. Recipients must be flexible and understand that weather and crop cycles may change what is available and when it will arrive. And cooks must be open to working with vegetables they have never cooked before.

In the summertime, the Up Island Council on Aging, one of four Island Councils on Aging, provides gleaned food to an estimated one hundred families every week. They offer a Surplus Food Program to people in need, and the gleaned food is a fresh, local addition.

But all seniors who visit the Council on Aging, regardless of income, have access to gleaned food when it's available. "A lot of people will come in and get things. And if it's the end of the week they'll take ten pounds of tomatoes, but they turn around and make a tomato paste or sauce and share it with people. They sell it at the local church bazaars, or donate it to a benefit for a family in need," says Ellen Reynolds, outreach coordinator for the Up Island Council on Aging. "So the food goes a lot further than just somebody's table."

BUY LOCAL—EAT WELL

✳

The Martha's Vineyard agricultural scene is growing and changing. To help you navigate your way through eating locally, we offer you this listing of all farms on the Vineyard, plus location and contact information.

✳

THE INFORMATION WAS COMPILED BY
Edible Vineyard MAGAZINE.

Ethan Valenti, field crew manager (center), with his summer staff.

THE ALLEN FARM
It Started with the Land

The Allen Farm, a hundred acres of rolling land in Chilmark, has been tended since 1762 by twelve generations of the Allen family. Clarissa Allen grew up on this land, and, with her husband, Mitchell Posin, and their son, Nathaniel, and his wife, Kaila, runs a sheep farm and operates a small and diverse shop on the farm.

Mitchell had worked on farms in western Massachusetts and southern Vermont before coming to Martha's Vineyard. to help a friend build his parents a summer home. At the end of the summer of 1975, he met Clarissa.

Clarissa remembers: "In the late '60s and early '70s, Mitchell and I were influenced by a significant cultural shift that encouraged stepping aside from the growing consumerist lifestyle that seemed to be defining our futures.

"At first we started gardening, and before long we had horses, goats, pigs, and sheep. Soon we settled on sheep and woolens.

"By the early '80s we were able to begin concentrating exclusively on agriculture and the rebuilding of our farm."

Along the way they restored the 1772 timber-framed farmhouse, fought a serious title challenge, rebuilt the property's iconic but tumbling stone walls, and reclaimed pastureland that had become overrun with brush and trees. Allen Farm is now an up-Island landmark, with a shop selling wool products and local meat and eggs. And Clarissa and Mitchell are important voices in the Island's "living local" movement.

"This kind of rocky, and hilly, glacial moraine is well suited to sheep farming. Generations of Allens left the Vineyard for other pursuits; some settling in Maine and into the Midwest, but always a member of the family maintained the Chilmark homestead.

"I grew up with the belief that land was important and something finite. This sensibility helped define me."

ISLAND FARMS

Aquinnah

7a Farms
3 Oonouhkoi Rd, Aquinnah
508-645-2165 / www.7afoods.com
Dan Sauer and Wenonah Madison
Farmers' Market: seasonal produce, flowers. Farm tours available by appointment.

Chilmark

The Grey Barn
22 South Rd, Chilmark
508-645-4854 / www.thegreybarnandfarm.com
Molly and Eric Glasgow
Farm store: organic: fresh milk, cheese and dairy, meats, and eggs.

Allen Farm Sheep and Wool
421 South Rd, Chilmark
508-645-9064
Clarissa Allen and Mitchell Posin
Farm store: organic: grass-fed lamb, beef, pork, pastured poultry, eggs, wool and wool products, organic fertilizer, compost tea.

Beetlebung Farm
Middle Rd at Beetlebung Corner, Chimark
508-645-2280
Marie Scott
Farm stand: vegetables, herbs, salad greens, flowers. June to October. Also sold at Farmers' Market.

Mermaid Farm and Dairy
9 Middle Rd, Chilmark
508-645-3492
Caitlin Jones and Allen Healy
Farm stand: heirloom tomatoes, garlic, vegetables, lamb, beef, raw cows' milk, yogurt, cheese, yarn. Also sold at Farmers' Market.

Murphy Blueberry Farm
8 Rumpus Ridge Rd, Chilmark
508-645-2883
Susan and Lynn Murphy
Farm: u-pick blueberries, by appointment.

Native Earth Teaching Farm
94 North Rd, Chilmark
508-645-3304
Rebecca Gilbert and Randy Ben David
Farm stand: eggs, seasonal berries, herbs, vegetables, plants; occasional chicken, pork, duck, and turkey. Farm tours, special events. Wed 10–6, Sat–Sun 10–6.

North Tabor Farm
4 North Tabor Rd, Chilmark
508-645-3331
Rebecca Miller and Matthew Dix
Farm stand: salad greens, shitake mushrooms, vegetables, eggs, flowers, honey, pork, poultry. Also sold at Farmers' Market.

The Shermans
Chilmark, Ralph and Ethel Sherman
Farmers' Market: seasonal produce, jams and jelly.

Blue Bird Farm
Tea Lane Farm, Tea Ln, Chilmark
774-563-8274
Krishana Collins
By appointment: wedding flowers, seasonal produce, greens. Also sold at Farmers' Market.

MERMAID FARM
Building for the Next Generation

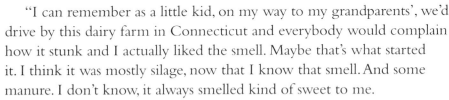

Allen Healy and Caitlin Jones have run a dairy on their farm in Chilmark since 2005. This was not the result of a grand plan. Caitlin's parents, Virginia Jones and Everett Jones, purchased the land in 1968. Caitlin moved there in the early '90s, soon to be joined by Allen.

From the time she was a child, if she wasn't climbing trees, Caitlin was growing plants. Allen, who has a background in aviation mechanics, had a talent for fixing things. Both had done farm work, but they didn't plan at first to farm their land commercially. They grew vegetables for themselves and eventually their sons, Kent and Everett, and they sold the extras by the side of the road.

The story of the dairy began with a dog. Caitlin and Allen got a border collie, and to train him they needed sheep. They got some sheep and have been raising them ever since. Events took their course, and in 2004 Allen bought the farm's first cows. They began selling their raw milk the following year. Now they have a small herd of dairy cows and sell raw milk, yogurt, cheese, and a mean mango lassi along with vegetables and wool at a very small self-serve farm stand on Middle Road.

Much of the land originally purchased by Caitlin's parents is now in permanent conservation. Allen, first using the small herd of sheep and then his motley collection of hand-me-down tractors, has helped restore and keep in agricultural production many acres of pastureland along Middle Road.

Allen recalls his own interest in farming:

"I can remember as a little kid, on my way to my grandparents', we'd drive by this dairy farm in Connecticut and everybody would complain how it stunk and I actually liked the smell. Maybe that's what started it. I think it was mostly silage, now that I know that smell. And some manure. I don't know, it always smelled kind of sweet to me.

"I'm trying to build the farm for the next generation, because there really wasn't anything here when I started. Now there's a farm here. The fields are greener, and there are animals along the road and there weren't before. Having two little kids dragging tools off into the woods is a real challenge, but it's getting there, it's slowly getting there. I just can't rush it."

ISLAND FARMS

Edgartown

Old Town Gardens
51 Road to the Plains, Edgartown
508-627-5827
Robert Daniels
Farm stand: organic vegetables, potatoes, flowers. Also sold at Farmers' Market.

The FARM Institute (Food, Agriculture, Resource Management)
Katama Farm, 14 Aero Ave, Edgartown
508-627-7077 / www.farminstitute.org
Farm stand: seasonal vegetables, eggs; grass-fed beef, pork, and lamb; pastured turkey for Thanksgiving. Year-round children's educational programs, summer farm camp, corn maze, and other special events focused on educating the community in sustainable agriculture. Also sold at Farmers' Market.

Morning Glory Farm
Edgartown-West Tisbury Rd, Edgartown
508-627-9003 / www.morninggloryfarmstand.com
Jim and Debbie Athearn, Simon Athearn, Daniel Athearn
Farm store: seasonal fruits and vegetables, corn, herbs, beef, pork, eggs, chicken, pies and other baked goods, plants. Mon–Sat 9–6, Sun 10–5. Also sold at Farmers' Market.

Slip Away Farm
Chappaquiddick, 199 Chappaquiddick Rd, Edgartown
508-627-7465 / www.slipawayfarm.com
Lily Walter, Christian Walter, Collins Heavener
Farm stand: seasonal produce, herbs. Also sold at Farmers' Market.

Oak Bluffs

Bayes Norton Farm
223 Edgartown-Vineyard Haven Rd, Oak Bluffs
508-696-5989
Jim and Sonya Norton, Jamie and Diane Norton
Farm stand: seasonal fruits and vegetables, herbs and more. Sun–Mon 9–6.

COMSOG (The Community Solar Greenhouse)
114 New York Ave, Oak Bluffs
508-693-2019 / www.mvgreenhouse.org
Thalia Scanlan
Self-serve greenhouse: seasonal vegetables, heirloom tomatoes and flowers; walks, tours, workshops, and clinics on topics of sustainable island gardening and natural plantings.

DeBettencourt's Farm
120 Wing Rd, Oak Bluffs
508-693-1520
Joanne and Kenneth DeBettencourt
Farm stand: seasonal vegetables and flowers.

Tisbury

The Good Farm
Tisbury Meadow Preserve
Martha's Vineyard Landbank Commission
508-627-7141 / www.thegoodfarmmv.com
Jefferson Monroe
To buy by appointment: pastured poultry. Also sold at Farmers' Market.

Bakehouse Farm
Scottish Bakehouse, 977 State Rd, Tisbury
508-693-6633
Zephir Plume
Farm stand: seasonal vegetables, flowers.

NORTON FARM
Carrying On a Family Tradition

In 1837 Bayes Norton, a sheep farmer, bought land on the Vineyard Haven/Oak Bluffs town line. He and his son farmed it until his son died in 1903. The farm landed in the hands of a man who carried the same family name but a different profession. This Bayes M. Norton was a professor and did not live year-round on Martha's Vineyard. He and his family spent summers on the island, but their land was fallow.

By 1972, when the land was reappraised in a tax change, Bayes's great-great-grandson Jim Norton managed the family property. Like his father, he was a professor off-island. Jim was suddenly faced with a life-altering decision. The only way for him to afford to keep the land was to actively farm it. And so he did. He and his family left the world of academia and moved full-time to Martha's Vineyard, he says, "to reactivate the family farm as a farm." He's philosophical about the career change, saying, "My function in farming is trying to create the healthiest environment I can for the plants we grow, in the hope that they'll produce the best they can. I don't think that's very different from what I was trying to achieve in the classroom."

Now, Jim and Sonya's son Jamie and his wife, Dianne, have taken over the vegetable farm on the outskirts of Vineyard Haven, where passing drivers keep an eye out each summer for the sign outside the farm stand announcing, "Our peas are in!" They are full-time teachers in the Island public schools, and in the summer, full-time farmers. Their young sons, Dougie and Jonathan, are, on their summer breaks from school, full-time farmers, too. And Jim Norton can concentrate now on his favorite task, cultivating the tomatoes.

"Both of us love teaching and feel it is something we were meant to do with our lives. However, farming has become part of who we are.

"The students and fellow teachers know we are farmers. We're the ones who carry cartons of eggs through the halls and bring in surplus veggies when the harvest is bountiful.

"It is important to us that the farm stays in the family. We won't be around forever, and it would be comforting to know that Dougie and/or Jonathan were ready (and happy) to take over. Knowing where you come from is important to keeping yourself grounded—knowing that you are a part of something bigger than yourself. That's what we would like to pass on to the boys as they grow up."

ISLAND FARMS

Down Island Farm
280 Takemmy Path, Tisbury
508-696-8447
Heidi Feldman and Curtis Friedman
To buy by appointment: edible flowers, herbs, shitake mushrooms. Also sold at Farmers' Market.

Northern Pines Farm
Northern Pines Rd off Lambert's Cove Rd, Tisbury
508-693-1025
Janet and John Packer
To buy by appointment: chicken, beef, pork.

Pilot Hill Farm
100 Pilot Hill Farm Rd, Tisbury
508-274-8706
Beldan and Dave Radcliffe
Farm stand: eggs, flowers, seasonal vegetables.

Spring Moon Farm
Northern Pines Rd off Lambert's Cove Rd, Tisbury
508-693-7354
Liz Packer and children
To buy at SBS Grain Store, 480 State Rd, Tisbury, and by appointment: Oscar's eggs, seasonal lamb, pork; piglets; wool: fleece, yarn, hides.

Thimble Farm (Island Grown Initiative)
Head of the Pond Rd, off Edgartown-Vineyard Haven Rd, Tisbury
office@islandgrown.org
Keith Wilda
Farm stand: seasonal produce, hydroponic greens, strawberries.

West Tisbury
The West Tisbury Farmers' Market
Grange Hall, State Rd, West Tisbury
508-693-9561 / www.westtisburyfarmersmarket.com
To buy at market: seasonal fruits and vegetables, honey, salad greens, bread, baked goods, jams and jellies, island products, flowers, plants. Wed 9–12, late June through August; Sat 9–12, June to October. Winter market starting in October at the Agricultural Hall.

Blackwater Farm
Lambert's Cove Rd (behind Cottle's Lumber), West Tisbury
508-693-9785
Debbie Farber and Alan Cottle
Farm stand: eggs, beef, pork, seasonal vegetables, flowers. Also sold at Farmers' Market. Feed and mulch hay by appointment.

Whippoorwill Farm
Old County Rd, West Tisbury
508-693-5995
Andrew Woodruff
Farm stand: seasonal vegetables, tomatoes. Also sold at Farmers' Market.

Breezy Pines Farm
164 Tiahs Cove Rd, West Tisbury
508-693-9573
Travis and Heather Thurber
Farm stand: seasonal vegetables, eggs and flowers. Sun–Mon 8–6, June through September. Chicken feeding, tours, children's summer gardening camp (August). Also sold at Farmers' Market, Wednesdays only.

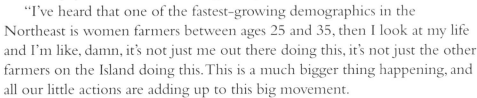

SLIP AWAY FARM
A New Wave of Young Farmers

Lily Walter took a summer job at the Morning Glory farm stand in her early college years—and fell in love with farming. Working summers through college at Morning Glory, she graduated to the post of field crew manager, and then set her sights on starting a farm of her own. In September 2012 Lily, her brother Christian, and friend Collins Heavener, moved into the old Marshall farmhouse on Chappaquiddick Island and began the venture that is now Slip Away Farm. It represents the first real, working agricultural operation on the small island in decades.

Slip Away Farm is a profoundly collaborative effort—involving not only the three farmers but also the Martha's Vineyard Preservation Trust, which owns and has restored the historic farmhouse, and the Martha's Vineyard Land Bank, which owns the land and, like other conservation groups on the Island, has begun to make conserved land available to farmers. All the farmers are also past employees of Morning Glory.

Time after time, Slip Away Farm has also been the recipient of generous support from a Chappy community that has rallied around the enterprise, lending farm machines and tools, pitching in to put up the new greenhouse, even contributing dollars to help upgrade the soil. As one Chappaquiddicker explained, "This is not just any rural activity we support, but one full of vitality, with the look of domesticity and prosperity inherent in a working farm. It's like a centrally located heart to the body of our Island—one that offers to feed us."

"I've heard that one of the fastest-growing demographics in the Northeast is women farmers between ages 25 and 35, then I look at my life and I'm like, damn, it's not just me out there doing this, it's not just the other farmers on the Island doing this. This is a much bigger thing happening, and all our little actions are adding up to this big movement.

"Here on the Island, there's a certain mentality of I'll help you out, you'll help me out, we're all in this together; to not see another farmer as competition, but to see them as a friend, a resource, and a support system. There are so many farmers on the Island who have been doing this for so long, who have been making it work for so long. It's so valuable to have those connections and to have those people as friends because they understand what it takes and what we're trying to do here. There's something really comforting in that—in knowing that Morning Glory started as a little umbrella on the side of the road, and forty years later has become what it has become."

ISLAND FARMS

Cleveland Farm
674 Old County Rd, West Tisbury
508-693-2043
Richard and Ina Andre
Farm stand: eggs, pastured poultry, pork.

Christiantown Farm
185 Christiantown Rd, West Tisbury
508-693-2065
Sam and Sue Hopkins
To buy by appointment: grass-fed lamb, eggs, seasonal vegetables.

Flat Point Farm
Road to Great Neck, off New Ln, West Tisbury
508-693-5685
Arnie Fischer Jr. and Eleanor Neubert
To buy by appointment: grass-fed lamb and beef, feed hay, pastured poultry.

Ghost Island Farm
27 Davis Look Rd, off State Rd, West Tisbury
508-693-5161
Rusty Gordon and Sarah Crittenden
Farm store: seasonal produce, flowers, eggs, Nip 'n' Tuck beef and pork, Island products. Also sold at Farmers' Market.

Nip 'n' Tuck Farm
39 Davis Look Rd, West Tisbury
508-693-1449
Fred Fisher III
Sold at Ghost Island Farm store: eggs, beef, pork.
To buy by appointment: mulch hay, feed hay, manure.

RunAmok Farm
200 Lambert's Cove Rd, West Tisbury
508-693-9957
Kate and Brian Athearn
Farm stand: eggs, seasonal vegetables, wool products.

Stannard Farms
Off Lambert's Cove Rd, West Tisbury
Lisa Fisher and Tommy Reynolds
Farmers' Market, Saturday only: certified organic vegetables, greens, herbs, garlic, eggs.

Stoney Hill Farm
196 Stoney Hill Rd, West Tisbury
508-693-9486
Glenn and Rosemary Jackson
Farm stand: eggs, seasonal vegetables. To buy by appointment: wool.

Tiasquin Orchard
Carl's Way, West Tisbury
508-693-0081
Carl Magnuson
To buy at Morning Glory Farm: Apples.

Up Island Eggs
29 Scotchmans Ln, West Tisbury
508-693-6065
Katherine Long
To buy at Alley's General Store: eggs
By appointment: chicken rearing consultation.

Green Island Farm
State Rd, West Tisbury
www.sixburnersue.com
Susie Middleton and Roy Riley
Farm stand: eggs, seasonal produce. Seven days a week, 8–7.

Whiting Farm
State Rd, West Tisbury
beawhiting@mac.com
Bea Whiting
To buy by appointment: lamb, poultry, pork.

ACKNOWLEDGEMENTS

Morning Glory's Farm Food owes a lot to many. Special thanks goes to all the Vineyarders who helped test recipes: Joan Chaput, Art Smadbeck, Jean, Bill, and Hunter Cleary, Melissa Hackney, Polly Brown, Wendy Jacobs, Jessica Barker, Betsey Mayhew, and Kimberly Angell.

Another round of applause goes to Catherine Walthers and Susie Middleton, professional chefs who generously shared their own recipes with us.

We would also like to thank Prudence Athearn Levy and Josh Levy, who shared recipes from their Edgartown-based nutritionist company, Vineyard Nutrition. And to *Edible Vineyard*, who gave us their list of Island farms for our Buy Local section.

Finally, these words from Gaby Redner:

"I am grateful to Jim, Debbie, Simon, and Dan Athearn, as well as the entire Morning Glory field, kitchen, and stand crews for taking the time during their busy season to have meaningful conversations and to share stories. Thank you to Dad, Jess, and all my family for your support and enthusiasm, and to Alex and Judy for your listening and inspiration. Thanks to Jan Pogue at Vineyard Stories for the opportunity to write this book, which made for a most memorable season. Thanks also to Harold McGee, for writing a food book that is agricultural and culinary and so much more."

—Many Thanks from the Athearn Families

Jim and Debbie

Robyn, Simon, Rose, and Ignatius

Josh, Prudence, Kyle, and Judah

Meeghan, Dan, Penelope, Clara, and Zebediah

INDEX